Adva

MW00476836

Unchain the Pain

"*Unchain the Pain* is a rare gift to those who have suffered emotional pain, which is all of us. Bob Livingstone has demystified the therapeutic process and given anyone willing to invest the time and energy a sound, empowering, step-by-step process for self-healing."
–Abby Seixas, psychotherapist and author of
*Finding the Deep River Within: A Woman's Guide
to Recovering Balance and Meaning in Everyday Life*

....

"I loved this fascinating book. It provides new tools for working through emotional trauma."
–Russell Friedman, author of
*The Grief Recovery Handbook, 20th Anniversary
Expanded Edition: The Action Program for Moving Beyond Death,
Divorce, and Other Losses including Health, Career, and Faith*

....

"As a psychologist in private practice for over 25 years I've found patients can do a lot to help themselves using their own power to heal, if given the right tools. Bob Livingstone's book, *Unchain the Pain: How to be Your Own Therapist*, shows readers how to ask the right questions and utilize the answers to find their way toward feeling better about themselves."   –Vivian Diller, PhD, author of
*Face It—What Women Really Feel
Like when their Looks Change*

....

"The program in the book holds the belief that we all have the power to heal ourselves."   –Jena Forrest, author of
Help Is On Its Way: A Memoir About Growing Up Sensitive

"We all have the answers to our questions within ourselves; this book provides an easy to follow process to find the answers we need in order to heal." –Madisyn Taylor, author of
DailyOM

....

"Bob Livingstone has written a powerful and practical book. *Unchain the Pain: How to be Your Own Therapist* is a book that will empower the reader, but does so with great patience and compassion; a book that offers wonderful hope and reassurance to heal and regain passion for life; a book that will be of enormous help to anyone who wants to make the most of their healing journey. So get a pen, or a blank page on your computer, and follow Bob's gentle guidance and wisdom. You will be glad you did. I highly recommend this book."
–Thomas Roberts, LCSW, LMFT, author of
The Mindfulness Workbook:
A Beginners Guide to Overcoming Fear and Embracing Compassion

....

"Want to pull yourself up by the bootstraps but don't exactly know how? *Unchain the Pain: How to be Your Own Therapist* shows you how to overcome chronic worrying, move beyond painful childhood issues, conquer feelings of emptiness and disappointment in yourself, and confront numerous other causes of psychological angst. You will learn how to access your internal wisdom and become your own best therapist. A must for those determined to make their life better!'
–Susan E. Carrell, author of
Escaping Toxic Guilt:
5 Proven Steps to Free Yourself From Guilt for Good!

....

"This innovative, beautifully written guide provides a simple process everyone can follow, along with specific questions to ask to uproot old patterns of anger, grief, or emotional pain and find happiness."
–Gracelyn Guyol, author of
Who's Crazy Here? Holistic Steps to Recovery for ADHD,
Addiction, Anxiety, Depression, Bipolar Disorder,
Schizophrenia and Autism

"I highly recommend this book and Bob Livingstone's work! I was captivated by every page. It gives the reader a sense of empowerment and control over their own emotional health issues."

–Chris Linnares, creator of
Diva Dance

Unchain
the
Pain

How to be Your Own Therapist

Bob Livingstone, LCSW

Printed in the United States of America
ISBN: 978-1-935254-59-1

Cover Design by Vorris "Dee" Justesen
Book Design by Nadene Carter

First printing, 2011

This book is dedicated to my partner,
lover, wife and best friend for almost forty years:
Gail Meadows.

Acknowledgements

I would like to thank
Sammie and Dee Justesen and Nadene Carter,
the staff at NorlightsPress.com,
my literary agent Kristin Goering,
editor and mentor Lou Aronica,
Norman and Sharon Kman,
Linda Camarena,
All my friends and family

Table of Contents

Introduction

I've been a psychotherapist in private practice for twenty-four years. During a session with one of my clients, I suddenly realized how much time I spent asking questions aimed at showing people how to discover insights about their emotional pain. I wondered, "What if I could somehow teach folks to ask their own questions? What if I could show people how to examine their emotional hurt without having a therapist in the room to guide them?"

This concept generated the idea for *Unchain the Pain*, a book that holds great promise for those interested in self-help.

In many cases, seeking a therapist is the most appropriate step to take. If you're suicidal or recently traumatized in some way, finding professional assistance is the course to follow. At other times, asking the right emotional pain question on your own will lead to insights, deep understanding, and peace of mind. I provide examples of this phenomenon throughout the book.

A thirty-five-year-old woman who was repeatedly raped as a child overcomes this trauma to become a leading saleswoman in computer software. A middle-aged man loses his beloved wife in a freak accident and learns to appreciate life once again. A thirty-year-old woman who was abandoned by her parents learns to love herself. A sixty-year-old man finally lets his guard down and learns to fully love his partner. Each of these people used the Inquire Within Program to identify, face, and work through emotional pain by learning to ask themselves the right questions.

We've been taught that we can only learn to understand what makes us tick by seeking help from teachers, politicians, therapists, celebrities, and other professionals. The Inquire Within Program shows we all have the power to heal ourselves and the wisdom to find answers to our most overwhelming questions. And yes, we can learn to tolerate the often tumultuous process of discovering answers to the hard questions.

Inquire Within is a new model for self-discovery and recovery from psychological wounds. I present this material to readers for the first time in *Unchain the Pain: How to be Your Own Therapist*. This is the first book that teaches how self-questioning can resolve internal conflicts and help you discover joy in your life.

If you are currently in treatment, Inquire Within can also be used to compliment psychotherapy. You can use the program to enhance your weekly therapy sessions by discovering new insights and understandings.

In the early chapters of the book you'll read more about the benefits of self-questioning, and I'll discuss issues that may be affecting your life as you consider trying this program. Since this is a new form of self-help, you may have questions and doubts -- and I will address those. From there we move toward preparation, as I show you how to overcome your natural fear of this self-analysis, how to train yourself to be a better questioner, and how to provide the proper environment for doing this work.

I will take you through a series of exercises, present case studies, and then lead you into the heart of the Inquire Within Program. The process requires commitment and bravery from all who participate, but the results can be dramatic and profoundly satisfying. Along the way, you will meet others who've been through this experience and you will learn from their discoveries.

The Inquire Within Program can transform dysfunctional states to elation. *Unchain the Pain* is a breakthrough book; a tool you can use to teach yourself the benefits of self-analysis and come away happier and filled with a new perspective on your life.

Special instruction: Please read the entire book before beginning the actual program that begins in Chapter Seven.

NOTES

Chapter 1
The Benefits of Self-Questioning

If you're like many people, you've already spent much of your life exploring self-help groups, receiving therapy, or following the latest trends that promise mental health and serenity. Perhaps you gained solace from these activities, but you still feel something is missing. Despite your best efforts, the people around you seem joyful, while your own good times are few and far between.

You wonder how it would feel to experience moments of bliss and contentment; to have an open, intimate relationship. What if you could love yourself and know for certain you're making a positive contribution to the world? What if you could go through a day without feeling anxious, fearful, or emotionally numb?

Perhaps you've resisted delving into your inner world. You believe self-exploration is a shallow invention of pop psychologists – a moneymaking tool for charlatans. And yet, at least a dozen times a day you find yourself feeling lonely, lost, and afraid. Your best efforts to achieve happiness have left you floundering. For the first time in your life you feel ready to step outside your self-created limitations and discover joy.

I'm glad you've chosen *Unchain the Pain* for this journey. Within these pages you'll find a dramatic and effective way to view your life and address the lingering issues that plague you. The heart of this method involves asking questions of yourself, much as a therapist or other trained professional would do.

What will you gain from exploring your life this way?

You will learn to be introspective.

Introspection is the ability to look inside for answers to the negative issues in your life. This simple tool allows you to ponder your role and the role of others in creating your problems. You'll learn to assess where you are in life emotionally, spiritually, and financially, and then look at your strengths, flaws, and weaknesses, and measure your personal growth.

Being introspective isn't always fun. This technique can be painful as you uncover secrets you've kept from yourself and raise issues your parents and others taught you to repress. You may be afraid of introspection because you've seen people in pain who became obsessed with their troubles and couldn't function. However, obsessing is different from introspection. Obsessing is dominated by circular, worry-filled thoughts. Being introspective involves asking yourself important questions in a calm, thoughtful way. Introspection allows you to face your issues without beating up on yourself or filling your heart with guilt.

You will discover how being introspective enriches your life.

If you never question why certain events happened in your life, how can you hope to learn or progress from these intense experiences? If you have difficulty maintaining close relationships and never ask yourself why a scenario tends to repeat itself, you will probably continue having relationships that abruptly end. Being truly introspective includes the question, "What role did I have in this issue?" At first, assessing your own accountability will feel threatening. These feelings will ease with practice.

In addition, you'll find yourself attracted to – and building strong connections with – other people who value introspection. Connecting with others may be our most essential task in life.

You will be more self-reliant and less dependent on others for approval.

As children, many of us learned to not ask for help; seeking assistance was seen as a sign of weakness – and weakness makes us vulnerable. But at this point in your life you may be resigned to asking other people for answers. Uncertain how to look inside, you turn to friends, parents, or other mentors to help you view yourself. "Do you think I'm smart?" "Am I a good baseball player?" "Do you think I'm attractive?" "Do I seem like a good friend?"

We learn to ask our confidants these questions instead of asking ourselves, because we believe others know the answers to these questions better than we do. We usually get positive answers that create a fleeting sense of well-being. This is like a drug that makes you feel euphoric for an hour. And, like a drug, it has an addictive quality. You feel a rush of excitement when someone confirms you're smart, nice looking, talented at sports, or a good friend.

Unfortunately, when these answers come from outside ourselves we don't internalize them. Positive comments and reassurance from other people are not ultimately fulfilling or satisfying because they don't compel you to rely on your internal resources, your inner strength, or your knowledge. Nor do they touch the way you truly feel about yourself.

You will learn to be more patient with yourself and others.

Many of us feel we should immediately find answers to our problems. When solutions don't come easily, we tend to push the question away. We lack the patience, tolerance, and perseverance to look hard at upsetting memories. Instead, we seek the quick fixes of mental Band-Aids or denial.

Learning to be with this discomfort is a major part of the Inquire Within Program. The first step is to accept the fact that finding answers is not an instantaneous process. When painful memories arise, you can accept that they will be hurtful until you work through them.

Please don't beat up on yourself for mentally running away from your problems. We all do it, because we're impatient with ourselves and sometimes ashamed of our feelings.

You probably learned to see problems as a disgraceful part of your personality. Shame is an ingrained belief that you committed an unforgivable act, which in turn causes you to think you're a bad person who doesn't deserve the best life has to offer. Shame convinces you that bad things happen to you because you're a bad person.

Patience is the ability and willingness to wait for healing to occur. When trying to address your emotional pain, it's important to realize that change takes time and your healing journey will not be linear. Using patience during this time can lead to a peace of mind you've never experienced. Being patient with yourself also allows you to feel more tolerant of others.

You will become emotionally unstuck.

Feeling stuck is the experience of being mired in psychological quicksand. Whatever your dilemma, you believe there's no way out for you. Spending enough time in this zone eventually leads to a state of numbness where you feel neither sadness nor joy. You pass through life like a robot, mindlessly going through the motions of your daily routine.

Being emotionally stuck is a reaction to upsetting events in your life that caused you to shut down. You lose the ability, and sometimes the desire, to connect with others. You consciously avoid taking risks that might improve your quality of life. You see no prospects for the future.

You see your job as a dead end. At work you show no initiative and appear to be slogging through each day, waiting for retirement, even if that goal is years away. You perform just well enough to get a satisfactory evaluation. You have no interest in personal relationships, either friendships or lovers. You aren't sure why you feel this way, but relationships seem like too much work.

Although you don't feel real sadness or anger, it is possible to get frustrated and hostile. You may lose your temper and destroy property, but have no insight about why you blew up. The immediate trigger is usually something like a driver cutting you off or a customer service representative showing no customer service skills. You're sitting on a smoldering pile of rage you displace on others.

The Inquire Within Program helps you become emotionally unstuck. You'll ask yourself questions that reveal what being emotionally stuck does to you and how you can free yourself.

You will be able to resolve long-standing emotional issues.

Many of us have long-standing emotional problems we may not recognize. These issues probably began in childhood and have affected you during most of your life. When we don't recognize the source of emotional pain, we tend to repeat dysfunctional acts, like choosing partners who are thoughtless, letting people take advantage of us, or continually self-sabotaging our own efforts to find happiness.

Emotional issues can keep you from forming and achieving personal and professional goals. They inhibit long-term, intimate relationships. They make you feel incomplete and you suffer from low self-esteem. You lack confidence and always believe tragedy is just around the corner. You have difficulty expressing anger and sadness in appropriate ways. You tend to lash out at others when you feel unjustly criticized. You feel as though you don't belong in any social setting, which contributes to feeling alienated from others. This state of isolation makes it difficult for you to make friends or even acquaintances.

If you're aware of what's bothering you, perhaps you've been afraid to face this pain, or you don't believe working on it will benefit your life. Unresolved, long-term emotional pain is often a major factor in drug or alcohol abuse. If your mind is flooded by overwhelming thoughts and feelings related to your struggles, you may be self-medicating to deal with the stress from these hidden problems.

Many of us learn to deal with longstanding emotional pain by repressing it and then deluding ourselves into believing the issues have vanished. But these unresolved issues tend to pop up in unexpected ways until we face them.

Asking yourself questions about your emotional pain allows you to build self-esteem. You begin demonstrating to yourself that you have the courage to tackle difficult issues that may reside in childhood. Inquiring within opens the door to painful memories you will learn to tolerate as you master this process. You'll begin to connect the dots and understand why you've had problems expressing yourself or being intimate, or why you always feel afraid. You will learn to change your beliefs, thoughts, and attitudes about these issues.

You will discover your place of wisdom.

Asking yourself questions about your emotional pain will help you discover your wise place. Asking the right questions may open the door to deep, soul-searching answers.

Many of us are cut off from our place of wisdom; the place that holds our truth. There, you can seek answers to the most troubling questions regarding your life. You can go there when you need solace, security, and self-love. Some call this the soul, while others call it God or Goddess.

Some people don't believe in anything that will help get them through the night. No afterlife, and no soul, God, or divine wisdom. Maybe we've lost our faith, or perhaps we never had any faith to begin with. Many of us are cynical and our hearts burn from the bitterness that goes along with this disparaging attitude.

Finding your place of wisdom doesn't require a religious or spiritual belief. You simply learn to have faith in yourself that you will persevere, survive whatever comes your way, and land on your feet. You learn to trust that life will show you the way through tough times and you will eventually discover peace of mind.

Having a place of wisdom allows you to rely on your own judgment. You can touch the deepest part of your pain and find the strength to endure. You begin to understand what trauma did to you and what you can do about it. You learn that no one knows you better than you know yourself. You learn to trust yourself, and then to trust others. You learn to love yourself, and then to love others. You let down your guard and experience joy.

You may find your place of wisdom while listening to a Marvin Gaye song or a Bruce Springsteen anthem. Music, sunsets, the ocean, or other moving experiences may open the door to your soul. You may have revelations about why you've been unhappy for so long and develop a plan to change your life. You may find your heart is open for the first time and you finally comprehend what love is. You may find yourself living in the present instead of worrying about the future or dwelling on the past. You feel alive and relaxed.

In order to get in touch with your place of wisdom, you must reach a point where you're willing to ask the hard questions about your emotional pain. You need to be prepared for feelings and memories that may be abhorrent, ugly, overwhelming, and frightening.

You will feel less depressed.

More than 18 million Americans suffer from depression. Depressed people are overwhelmed by hopelessness, guilt, anxiety, and sadness. This burden of negative feelings keeps them from focusing on a plan to improve their emotional health. Among other symptoms, depression causes loss of appetite or overeating, insomnia or excessive sleeping, loss of energy, and problems with relationships, work, and school.

Unfortunately, many people feel guilty about being depressed and seeking help. If you're in this category and can find the energy to learn the Inquire Within Program, you will keep your vulnerability private.

If you learn to explore your emotional world through self-questioning, at some point you may feel safe enough to discuss your issues with other people. Sharing your stories with friends, workshop members, colleagues, and therapists will let you know you aren't alone. You'll feel less isolated and withdrawn. As you connect with others, you'll gain confidence and self-esteem.

You will be able to work through grief and loss issues.

Grief and loss issues are difficult to face and work through. Our culture places a time limit on how long we're expected to show feelings of grief and talk about our loss. If you lose a loved one through death, you get a week or so of bereavement leave from work. Then you're expected to return and perform at the highest level. You're allowed to be sad at the funeral, but after that society sends you the message it's time to let go of your anguish and bear down. Your grieving period is officially over.

No two people grieve exactly the same way. Some of us are stoic and keep our own counsel, while others reach out to friends and family. If you're unable to work through grief, you may experience physical problems such as headaches and stomachaches. You may feel as though a heavy cloud keeps you from moving forward. You may be afraid to face your loss. This repression of feelings causes you to shut down and feel dead inside. Internal deadness is the experience of feeling nothing at all; you don't experience sadness, real anger, or joy.

The Inquire Within Program can help you overcome the fear of facing and working through a loss. You can learn to formulate questions about your grief. You can ask questions to determine if you are grieving, or if you need to mourn.

You will be less anxious.

Anxiety disorders are the most common mental illnesses in the United States, affecting forty million adults. Unlike depression, which is largely untreated because of shame and ignorance, people with anxiety are likely to misidentify their emotional upheaval as a physical ailment such as a heart attack. They head to the emergency room of their nearest hospital for intervention.

Asking questions about your emotional state at the onset of anxiety can be tremendously helpful. Your usual way of dealing with anxiety may be to elevate the fear by increasingly worried thoughts. You may begin this process by having a nervous stomach, increased heart rate, a feeling of impending doom, or hyperventilating. Worried thoughts exacerbate the anxiety, and you only find relief after the worry has run its course or you're too exhausted to continue this emotional tornado.

Inquire Within teaches you to interrupt this process by asking yourself questions such as, "Why am I having this panic attack" or, "What is happening right now that causes me to worry incessantly?" You learn to start asking these questions as soon as the overwhelming anxiety is about to begin. Discovering answers to these questions will eventually lead you to a calmer state, and you can learn ways to stop anxiety in its tracks.

Asking questions about your anxiety also helps after the intense worry fades away. During the throes of an anxiety attack, you may not be able to focus on questions, but later, when you get to a calm place, you can ask: "What was happening right before I started to worry?" The answer may be a surprising revelation and give you the confidence to move forward.

You will feel more confident and your self-esteem will increase.

Those of us who suffer from low self-esteem and lack of self-confidence tend to hang onto this dismal image of ourselves. We accept our perceptions as fact. We're also inclined to keep this private, not sharing our feelings with lovers, family, friends, or work acquaintances.

What if we decide the time has come to confront our negative self-images and all the heavy baggage that comes from long-term self-loathing? What if we begin to confront this rigid belief system by asking serious questions about why we feel this way, who's responsible, and how we can deal with our feelings?

The questions you ask will help you understand why you feel so negative about yourself. You'll learn to comprehend the damage done to you at an early age by parents and other authority figures. You'll find appropriate ways to express those bad feelings. You'll also learn to discern what behavior you're actually accountable for and what issues belong to others. Then you can begin to forgive yourself for living in your own private hell for so many years.

You will learn what it means to process your feelings.

Processing your feelings is a way to explore the emotional, intellectual, physical, and spiritual aspects of yourself. Processing is often seen as a feminine way of dealing with daunting personal issues. In our society women have the freedom to spend time discussing feelings and problems. Men aren't supposed to talk about troublesome topics, and they're definitely expected to ignore issues that get in the way of earning money.

This societal dictate keeps the stereotyped roles of men and women alive. Women are seen as weak and whimsical in their quest to chat with other females about issues. Men are supposed to be reserved and stoic. Today, men are allowed a bit more leeway and women have more leadership positions, but the basic roles of men and women haven't changed drastically since the 1950s.

While going through the Inquire Within Program, you will learn that men and women feel pain equally, and that working through our emotional issues takes time. Rushing to find immediate answers doesn't work. Processing involves asking yourself a series of personal questions that eventually lead to peace of mind and understanding. This way of looking at yourself is different from talking with others about your problems.

Inquire Within shows you how we each hold the answers to our own questions. This program asks you to trust that no one knows us better than we know ourselves. If we address our own questions honestly, we will find our own answers.

Within these pages I'm offering you something new: a process that will take you beyond every self-help method you've tried before.

Chapter 2

*Are You Ready to Begin
the Program?*

Y ou're a perfect candidate for Inquire Within if you
recently lost something important in your life, such as
your employment or your home. Perhaps you experienced the
death of a loved one, a breakup with a partner, or the end of a
friendship. Even the death of a beloved pet can be traumatic.

You're also a perfect candidate for Inquire Within if you feel
exhausted and pessimistic about the future. As time goes on,
the pain inside you feels worse instead of better. You're unclear
why this is happening and not sure what to do. You spend much
of your time blaming yourself for everything bad in your life.
You've thought of seeking help, but you're so worn down by the
stress of self-hatred that you can't even begin.

Some people believe you must be in a positive space to begin
a self-help program. Hell, if you were in a positive place, you

wouldn't need help. You're ready to begin the Inquire Within Program if...

You're tired of feeling unfulfilled and empty.

Can you remember the last time you were involved in an emotionally rewarding activity? At one time your life seemed more exciting and hope was in the air, but you were much younger and hadn't suffered hardships. Since then, tragedies and abusive relationships have piled up. Inside your mind you lack the tools to deal with these issues.

Now, when you look inside yourself you see an empty vessel. This emptiness causes you to feel depressed, useless, and without energy. During brief moments of clarity you understand you have a choice to continue this way of life or develop an alternative plan, but mostly you're too despondent to think about anything beyond survival.

When you become sick and tired of living a life that's going nowhere, find the motivation to change. Instead of using your rage to beat yourself up, use it to help you crawl out of the hole you've buried yourself in. When you reach the crawling out stage, you're ready for the Inquire Within Program.

Your life is so routine that brushing your teeth is the highlight of the day.

At this point in your life you're just going through the motions. Every task is a slow, torturous ritual: getting up in the morning, driving to your job, working, making small talk, and finally going to bed.

We reach this kind of plateau for several reasons. First, we learn about life by observing our role model parents. If our parents led boring lives, we're likely to do the same. Some people follow this lifestyle because the drudgery of a dull routine feels safe. Finding a better job, traveling, making friends, or starting a new hobby are threatening. If you risk doing something different you may lose whatever security you've accumulated.

If you live a tedious life, you probably have only a few friends because you live with a tremendous fear of being abandoned. If you're married, you and your partner may do tasks together well, but show little affection and avoid sharing your innermost dreams and fears. Anxiety about abandonment drives this as well. The thought of being left by someone you love is too much to even consider.

When you realize you're tired of being limited by your own fear of abandonment, you are ready for the Inquire Within Program.

Your anxiety creates worry everywhere you turn.

Are you constantly worried or on edge? Do you cling to fear you can't let go of, even though you know it isn't rational? Do you follow certain rituals throughout the day to prevent something horrific from occurring? Do you avoid situations because they make you nervous? Do you experience panic attacks that involve hyperventilating, racing heart, sweating, and feeling as though the room is closing in?

If you have any of these symptoms, you may be suffering from anxiety. Anxiety can be caused by environmental factors such as family dynamics, or trauma such as surviving a natural catastrophe. Genetics or brain chemistry may also cause anxiety.

Perhaps the constant worry is more than you can bear and you've decided to explore options. You consider seeing a psychiatrist and trying anti-anxiety medication. You've watched ads for these pills on late-night television when you can't sleep, but the side effects sound horrific. You don't want to suffer from depression, suicidal thoughts, increased anxiety, or sexual dysfunction. You have enough problems as it is. Therapy sounds like a good idea, but you don't have the money for this service right now.

If that's the case, you're ready for Inquire Within. This program allows you to help yourself by asking emotional pain questions that can help lessen your anxiety.

You feel emotionally numb much of the time and can't find excitement in any activity.

If you feel emotionally numb – no real sadness, no authentic anger, and no joy – you may be suffering from depression. The heavy weight of depression keeps you from fully expressing your feelings and prevents you from resolving your emotional pain. If you can't feel what you've lost, how can you possibly work through it?

If you find yourself sleeping too much or too little and not enjoying activities that used to bring you happiness; if you're eating too much or too little, withdrawing from others, and everything appears hopeless, you may be suffering from depression. You may have been depressed for years without being aware of it. Like anxiety, depression can be caused by genetics or environmental factors. Therapists use medication or psychotherapy to treat depression, but perhaps these options don't appeal to you right now.

You feel powerless, wrapped up in a victim blanket.

You blame everyone else for your troubles. Some days you want to be productive, but find yourself going back to bed. Your thoughts are filled with how useless everything is and how no one is there for you.

If you want to deal with this hopeless state that threatens to suffocate you, then you're ready for the Inquire Within program. By asking yourself the right questions, you will finally have an opportunity to see how you got here and connect the dots of your emotional unraveling.

You can't remember the last time you felt passionate about any aspect of life.

When your friends speak with enthusiasm about their latest projects, a new class they're taking, or a new person they met, you suddenly feel lost. You can barely imagine feeling excited or passionate about any aspect of life. Your limited emotional range moves from indifference to annoyance, with an occasional release through sex or exercise, although you don't especially enjoy either of these activities. Each time, before you have sex or exercise, you hope you'll find that spark of excitement you witness in friends, but this type of high never happens for you. When you go to a movie with a female friend and the film moves her to tears, you don't know how to act. You intellectually understand the film is sad, but you don't connect with the emotional drama on the screen.

You want to feel more, because you realize you may be missing out on much of what life has to offer. On the other hand, you fear opening up and being hurt. You desperately want to avoid being emotionally wounded, but you don't know why you feel this way.

You are ready for the Inquire Within Program when you realize you're missing vital aspects of life. You're tired of having a limited emotional range and exhausted from beating yourself up over your shortcomings. You want to be one of those people who cultivate deep friendships and loving partnerships.

The compromised state of your mental health affects your physical health.

You're tired of making appointments with your primary care physician for various aches and pains. You may have pain in your neck, stomach, shoulders, and other locations. When your doctor runs tests, they always come out negative. The doctor tells you nothing physical is causing your afflictions. You conclude the physical pain must be caused by stress.

You've been grinding it out at an unreal pace for a number of years now. No matter how hard you work, no matter how much energy you put into your kids' lives, you believe you're doing a poor job in all areas. You feel your work performance is substandard, even when you receive glowing evaluations. You worry about being disconnected from your children's lives because you don't have time to focus on their homework and activities.

You'd like to explore psychotherapy, but feel you don't have time for appointments right now. You barely find time to talk with your family each day. How on earth could you manage an hour-long appointment with a therapist?

When you reach this stage, you're ready for the Inquire Within Program. You'll find how to carve out time to work on your emotional health and do so at a pace that seems both deliberate and productive.

You have difficulty expressing anger and you're tired of being unable to release the rage boiling inside.

You are a father and husband with a solid career, but you've reached a time in your life where you realize you no longer express, or even recognize, anger. In fact, you purposely avoid any situation that could make you enraged. You're almost afraid of anger. Sometimes you feel a twinge of annoyance, but you hold it down. What if this alien feeling takes over your mind and causes you to lose control? You might utter a hurtful comment you can't take back. You might even get carried away and physically assault someone.

However, ignoring these feelings causes you to see yourself as a coward. You aren't being assertive enough, which hurts your self-image. You constantly criticize yourself about this. By not allowing anger to surface, you aren't sure how you feel about certain situations or people in your life. When you repress the anger, you also squelch all strong positive feelings. You're beginning to realize you may be cheating yourself out of the fullness of experience.

If this is the case, it's time to try the Inquire Within Program. Through this program you can finally ask yourself questions that reveal why you feel deep anger and why you try so hard to avoid these feelings.

If you find yourself in any of these situations, or something similar to one of them, I'm convinced the Inquire Within Program will enrich your life. Let's move forward and explore the program together.

NOTES

Chapter 3

*Overcoming Obstacles As You Begin
to Inquire Within*

Y ou've decided to take a huge step forward in your life and
explore the Inquire Within Program. Congratulations
on this positive decision! I believe you'll find this program
rewarding and well worth your time. However, you may
experience a few predictable obstacles.

Fear of Failure

Fear of failure could be your first hurdle. A little voice from
inside may tell you, "This program can't possibly work for me.
I'll be wasting my time and energy." This type of fear keeps us
from pursuing goals that will help us feel enlightened, fulfilled,
and at peace.

Has life beaten you down until you know you're destined to
fail? Have you experienced more than your share of bad luck?

Perhaps you've been on the losing end when it comes to career, family, friends, and relationships. In our culture we tend to view failure as a shameful experience, not a rite of passage. It seems we each get one shot at success, and if we don't make it we're a dismal failure. Fortunately, this is only a myth created by our high-pressure society.

Changing old, familiar patterns always involves a certain amount of risk and anxiety. But without taking risks how will you ever learn new things, find great relationships, win an exciting job, or make a new friend?

Many people grow up with role models who send negative messages: "You'll never succeed no matter how hard you work," or "There's no use trying, because people like us don't have a chance."

Perhaps your parents didn't support you and constantly put you down. You desperately tried to win their approval, only to be laughed at, scorned, or ignored. Some parents don't realize part of their job is to instill confidence in children, not tear down their self-esteem. These parents most likely didn't get any support during their own childhood, so they recycled this dysfunctional child-rearing style. Emotional abuse and lack of support take a huge toll on a child. If you grew up in such an environment, you were beaten down and never developed faith in your own abilities.

One way to overcome this emotional pain is to reach out to a mentor who will help you repair the damage. A mentor can provide kindness, guidance, and perhaps the unconditional love you've never experienced. You may need to make several attempts before you connect with a mentor you can actually trust. Because your parents have not been role models for nurturing adults, you won't be sure what you're looking for. Those of us who've been abused and or neglected tend to believe experiences with others will be either terrible or ideal. This mindset leaves no room for a middle ground. Such a belief system can lead to massive disappointment until you realize life is not all black or white; that there is a huge amount of gray. A caring mentor can teach you that imperfection is okay, and you don't have to jump through hoops to be loved. The Inquire Within Program is constructed to act as a mentor for you.

Fear of the Past

The second obstacle you may face is the valid fear that asking questions will unleash bad memories. It's true – if you choose to follow the Inquire Within Program, ugly memories and images may enter your conscious mind. But in Chapter 7 you'll learn to find and use an internal safe space where negative feelings can be neutralized. Using this technique allows you to move away from overwhemling memories and avoid feelings you choose not to face at a particular moment.

As you feel ready to deal with memories and the feelings attached to them, you'll learn to tolerate the discomfort they bring up. You'll understand that facing these memories allows you to work through what happened to you. Each successful step in working through your emotional pain will give you confidence to keep going.

Another confidence builder is to think back on life experiences when perseverance helped you achieve success. We often don't give ourselves credit for the the good things we've done, which might include being there for a friend in need, getting through school during a tough period of life, working at a dead end job to take care of your family, doing backbreaking menial work, providing for yourself when your parents weren't there for you, and having the courage to ask for help when doing so clashes with your value of total independence.

Tell yourself, "I've already overcome serious obstacles in my life, so I know I have the strength to face the ugly memories I'll encounter as I use the Inquire Within Program."

Emotional pain is often caused by internal conflict, and our society teaches us extreme, unhelpful ways to deal with this conflict. One method is to turn away from anything that feels painful. Many families have an unwritten rule to avoid all conflict. In this environment, admitting you have a problem implies you're weak and can't handle pressure. Other families and groups deal with external conflict by using violence toward their percieved enemies. Our society tells us that vulnerability equals weakness, which means you don't meet the standards for the All Powerful Man or the Do-it-All-Woman.

It's essential you begin to see internal conflict and emotional pain as a normal part of life, not a weakness or flaw that must be hidden from yourself and others. As you follow the Inquire Within Program, you'll find it liberating to acknowledge you're challenged by dealing with the loss of a loved one, divorce, being the victim of domestic violence, or being rejected by a long-term partner.

Fear of Unleashing Monsters

The third obstacle to overcome is a fear that self-questioning will uncover terrible things. Many people believe looking inward will unleash a monster. For that reason, some of us spend a lot of time and energy avoiding our own psyches. We believe we're supposed to be happy and sunny all the time, so when the sun fades in our lives we construct internal walls to hide the darkness within.

Thinking about all this creates shame, which leads us to push negative feelings away. But what is the truth here? Isn't the world composed of good, evil, and multiple shades of in-between? Do you believe whatever happens outside us is also incorporated inside us?

We all have demons. Many of them are caused by trauma, such as being abandoned by your parents, suddenly losing your job, being betrayed by your best friend, or losing a beloved pet. These demons create fear, anxiety, sadness and other feelings that may be triggered by memories or everyday events. Fortunately, you can learn to deal with unpleasant emotions by facing them. We conquer demons not by hiding from them, but by embracing them.

Within ourselves, we each have a deep well of calmness, great wisdom, and the infinite capacity to love. Those of us who've been traumatized have trouble maintaining a sense of calmness because we feel the need to constantly scan the horizon for possible threats to our security. Over time, this monitoring becomes an ingrained mental process – a habit. This troubling habit can be broken with practice and patience.

Blaming Others

The next obstacle to finding success from Inquire Within comes from blaming others for your problems and never feeling responsible for your shortcomings. Casting blame on others lets you maintain a sense of victimhood. Yes, you were hurt, abused, or discarded by others. But things will never get better if you continually blame someone else for your inability to improve your own life.

An example of this is a woman who was raped as a teenager. Now in her thirties, she blames the rape for her inability to form long-term relationships with men. She feels depressed and anxious much of the time. The rapist is certainly responsible for the harm he inflicted upon this woman years ago, but now he's gone from her life. She must take responsibility for her future, which includes dealing with things that happened over fifteen years ago. When she's ready to face her fear, the woman does a Google search for rape support groups in her area and finds a therapist who specializes in the trauma of rape.

Another example of being immersed in victimhood is an African-American man doing time in jail for drug possession with the intent to sell. He blames the racist criminal justice system for his arrest and conviction. He can pontificate for hours on the evil system and how it institutionalizes racism. Yet, this knowledge doesn't help him escape the revolving door of prison. He needs to get serious about his drug addiction and look inward for answers to his problems. He should utilize all the programs jail can offer, including help with substance abuse, classes toward his GED, and individual therapy. If these services aren't available in jail, he'll be able to find them once he's out.

If you believe other people are responsible for your problems, following the Inquire Within Program may be a challenge. Perhaps it's time to take charge of your own life.

Low Self-Confidence

The next obstacle is lack of self-confidence. Verbal abuse from parents, teachers, and other authority figures may have caused you to shut down your feelings. Now you believe opening up to others will lead to further pain and criticism. This unconscious thought process happens because as a child, when verbal abuse occurred, no adult intervened to help you work through the emotional wounds. No adult came to your defense when a teacher degraded you. Your parents seemed unaware you had emotional needs. They realized you were sensitive, but saw this trait as a liability. Their job was to transform you into a human turtle with a hard shell. However, you didn't want to be a turtle and had no idea how to toughen up.

Lack of self-confidence hinders you in establishing friendships, primary relationships, and obtaining an education. These feelings of low self-worth also create a sense of hopelessness and defeat. Although your insecure feelings may try to convince you this program can't help, Inquire Within will show you how to increase your confidence and self-esteem.

Passive Attitude

The next obstacle to overcome is being passive in your own healing process. Perhaps you expect people in the health care industry to heal your emotional pain without your input. Physicians, therapists, and healers are supposed to find solutions to your misery while you wait for results. These caring people may provide you with direction and warmth, but you need to perform the actual work. The price for healing includes a willingness to approach and process painful feelings and memories. Each step of the Inquire Within Program will help you leave this passive attitude behind and feel more in control of your life.

Distractions

The final obstacle to overcome is learning to block distractions that get in the way of emotional healing. We all have "must do" things in our lives: school, work, family obligations, and household chores. Your hyper-focus on these activities can turn into a way to avoid personal growth. Becoming too focused doesn't help you actually improve any of these functions. In fact, it may decrease your effectiveness, because hyper-focusing usually shows you're anxious about work, school, or raising your kids. The anxiety you feel doesn't come from the problems themselves; it comes from worrying that you won't measure up in these areas. Learning to separate problem solving from anxiety may be part of your work here.

Drama in relationships is another distraction. Frequent dramatic scenes are time-consuming, a waste of adrenaline, and ultimately leave you unfulfilled. You may also have self-destructive addictions to substances and to people who prevent you from focusing on your issues.

I'm not asking you to overcome all these obstacles before you start the Inquire Within Program. Becoming aware of them is the first step, and going through the program can help with each of the issues mentioned here. Remember, there's no such thing as perfection. If you're motivated to try this program, I encourage you to turn the page.

Chapter 4

*How to Develop and Nurture the
Self-Questioning Part of Yourself*

*A*certain amount of training is involved before you're
ready to use the Inquire Within Program. The first task
is to fine-tune your curiosity. Let's begin with a few questions:

Are you in touch with the inquisitive side of yourself?

Do you believe it exists or has a purpose?

Do you feel that being inquisitive is a valuable trait?

Do you ever question your long-held beliefs?

What happens inside you when you begin to question your
routine or a long-held conviction?

Do you allow yourself to pursue this avenue of thinking or
do you push it away?

We're all born with natural curiosity about how the world
functions. Asking questions is as natural as smelling, tasting,

or breathing. Matter of fact, being inquisitive is a major way children and adults learn new concepts, ideas, and formulations. This human trait leads to an important component of high-level mental activity: critical thinking.

The Power of Critical Thinking

Questioning yourself and others is a main feature of critical thinking. Critical thinking means questioning what you see and hear instead of automatically believing everything you're told, whether it comes on the news or from your boss. Critical thinking provides a window to the world that questions authority and rules. This viewpoint promotes change and is a force against personal and political stagnation. If you never question anything, your life will be based on fear, always wondering if edicts brought down by your parents, teachers, or bosses are fair. You also miss the opportunity to learn how to confront these rules in a productive manner.

Can you remember a student in one of your classes who wasn't afraid to ask dumb questions? Did you feel embarrassed for him, or angry because his questions used too much class time? Or did you secretly have the same concerns, but felt embarrassed to speak up yourself?

Asking questions and absorbing the answers is an enriching, exciting experience. If this is a void in your life, are you aware of what you're missing and how it affects you?

While it appears curiosity is a trait welcomed by American society, critical thinking and curiosity are not popular with the people in charge. On the one hand we're given the message that individualism is a worthy trait, while on the other hand, reality shows us we may be punished for thinking – and acting – outside the mainstream. Our culture idolizes pioneers and rugged individualists, yet it seems those in power wish for a dulled-down work force that fears being unemployed and is reluctant to challenge the status quo. In most organizations, you move up faster and further if you play strictly by their rules.

This form of social control is passed on to parents, who then teach their children to play the game. The game is all about not making waves, not questioning decisions that affect you, and maintaining a cool demeanor by not displaying anger.

This unwritten rule is worshiped on an intense level in contemporary America. During this time of financial uncertainty, large scale unemployment, and the high cost of education, parents often preach the "playing the game" slogan. In a world where competition for jobs and educational opportunities has greatly increased, parents often act out of panic.

They teach their kids that playing the game means smiling most of the time, making believe you're in total agreement with decisions made by your employer or teacher, and coming up with so-called solutions that match what you believe the boss or teacher wants.

While playing the game may lead to financial reward, what price do you pay by following this unwritten rule? This process leads to repression of thoughts and feelings. Questioning is a natural part of being human, yet this trait is constantly discouraged. This part of us gets pushed down and compartmentalized deep inside us. Compartmentalization is the process of placing uncomfortable information in a part of the brain that doesn't have access to the distress.

This repression can take the form of pushing anger away. But does your anger actually vanish? No, and it may resurface as debilitating depression. You may find yourself losing interest in activities that once gave you joy. You may find your mood is often dismal and you feel hopeless about the future. You may have difficulty sleeping or sleep too much. You may have no appetite or overeat.

Self-censoring your critical thinking may also have a negative effect on your imagination. It can stunt your sense of wonder. If you can't imagine, how can you dream about what's possible for you? If you can't imagine yourself as a great writer, how will you ever become one? If you don't wonder how it would feel to date that exciting man who lives down the hall, how will you ever find a spark in your relationships?

Playing the game can take its toll on nearly every aspect of your existence. While learning to get along in society is important for survival, we also need the ability to question ourselves and others, including our own beliefs. This questioning needn't be displayed in a rage, although you may feel angry about things that are forced upon you.

If you believe it's risky to question the status quo, how does that idea affect your intelligence and ability to reason? How will your mind expand with knowledge and new concepts if you don't question? You can learn to memorize facts and figures. You can spit out information in tests and for your employers, but this process isn't based on a love of learning. Memorizing is not a reflective process, nor does it leave room for what you think or feel about the material you've learned.

Inability or unwillingness to question may affect your ability to deeply connect with others. How can you develop more than a superficial relationship with a friend or partner if you cannot question that person's feelings, beliefs, and motives? Perhaps you're afraid of rejection if you ask tough questions. Maybe you have no idea how to begin the process because it feels like a foreign way to communicate.

Questioning can lead to deep connections with other people, creating the richest experiences in our lives. Questioning shows you have genuine concern for another person's thoughts and feelings. The warmth of that concern increases your joy. Questioning can help create a loving bond that becomes your guiding force. Knowing you are unconditionally loved and your back is always covered is a beautiful thing and makes you feel whole and secure in the world.

Questioning yourself about the need for love in your life can be painful, honest, and fulfilling. Failing to ask questions to uncover your need for affection and tenderness can lead you to become bitter and morose. We all have a primary need to be social and communicate with others. We want and need love from our friends and family. Questioning others as well as yourself can move you closer to them.

Conflict

If you don't practice asking questions of yourself or others, you'll have difficulty resolving conflicts. If a partner says something you perceive as offensive, you may feel hurt and angry. If you don't have the willingness or skill to ask your partner why she said these words, you may find yourself with no way to discuss the situation. Instead of asking questions about her comments, you may blow up in a rage that leads to the downfall of your relationship.

You also may perpetrate passive-aggressive behavior toward your partner, which is the act of showing anger in hidden ways, without being straightforward. For example: You're pissed off because your partner accused you of being mean to her. Instead of asking why she feels that way and attempting to resolve this pain, you give her the silent treatment and "forget" to wash the dishes for a whole week. When she says she believes you're avoiding the dishes because you're mad at her, you reply that she's wrong, you've just been too busy.

Here's another example: Your husband teases you in front of friends and hurts your feelings. Instead of asking why he feels the need to tease, you give him the silent treatment and avoid having sex with him. If he doesn't notice, you grow angrier. When he forgets to run an errand, you finally blow up and start an argument.

In both of these examples, your partner has no idea what's going on. If you asked probing questions and listened to the answers, you might grow closer instead of arguing.

If you don't self-question, you will also have problems resolving conflicts within yourself. If part of you wants to control all aspects of life, while another part of you is content to let life take its course, you can experience an intense internal conflict. This conflict can move back and forth between two extremes without ever having the two viewpoints intersect and join for resolution. If you don't ask questions about this phenomenon, you may not discover your conflict originates from abuse that occurred when you were a child. Moving between these two worlds can keep you in a state of misery.

Children Ask "Why?"

Asking questions is a natural aspect of human development. Children begin to inquire about the things around them as soon as they can talk, because being curious is a primary means of learning. Children ask about everything: "Why is the sky blue? What makes rain? Why does your face look like that?"

If questioning is discouraged or mostly ignored, how will learning take place for children, teens, and adults? The answer is simple: learning will not occur through rote memorization, but only through our natural inquisitive tendencies.

Out of expediency, many parents complete tasks for their children instead of creating an environment where kids use internal resources to solve problems and master the skills for academic and household chores. Children and parents are under great pressure to perform well at work and school, leaving scant time for teaching young people how to think, question, and problem solve on their own.

Here's another factor that teaches children not to ask questions, but to depend on their parents for virtually everything: Parents choose their kids' friends and plan activities with them through play dates. Parents drive children from one activity to another, living a hectic, stress-filled schedule. They compete with other parents for private schools, summer camps, and specialized tutors.

This all happens for families who have the financial means to pursue a luxurious life style. On the other hand, less affluent families have few economic or educational possibilities. These children either get lost in the system or don't have the luxury of learning to ask questions. Other young people become part of the prison system where their lives are totally orchestrated by those running the jails.

Children's natural inquisitiveness needs to be fostered, not repressed. Parents need to fight against society's message of, "Never rest, always think about moving up. If you aren't perfect you'll perish. Happiness is only possible if you attain material goals." A child's need for happiness and security gets lost in this mode of thinking.

Parents who set up a home environment that promotes questioning, critical thinking, and healthy debate will help not only enrich their children's lives, but also help themselves use and relearn skills they may have repressed. Parents may once again come to value these learning tools and realize a more fulfilling life.

Questions Can Help in a Crisis

When faced with a situation that feels uncomfortable, overwhelming, or outside your life experience, you may resort to several maladaptive practices that keep you from thinking clearly about the issues. For example, if you're suddenly laid off from your job you may become angry and destroy property, physically hurt someone, or turn to reckless behavior that might harm your own body. You may also become so anxious and worried you can't focus on finding another job. You might shut down and fall into a deep depression that keeps you from seeing alternatives.

Instead of becoming consumed by the initial inner terror, you might calm yourself by asking questions:

How much money do I have in savings and how long could I live on that money?

Who could help me find a job?

Who can tell me if this layoff is temporary or permanent?

Where do I apply for unemployment compensation?

Where can I obtain help for dealing with my overwhelming feelings?

These questions will help you to develop an action plan and overcome your sense of powerlessness. This doesn't mean all will be bliss, but you can create a sense of empowerment that didn't exist during the awful moment when you first knew you'd lost your job.

What if someone close to you unexpectedly dies? Your first reaction may be shock, numbness, hysteria, gut-level crying, screaming, or a sense that it didn't really happen. Whatever your initial feelings, asking yourself questions is a great beginning to the grieving process. You might ask:

Why do I miss her so much?

Why am I having so much difficulty expressing deep sadness about her loss?

Why can't I cry?

These questions, while initially painful, can help you find a place in your heart to hold your loved one, while freeing you to move on with your life.

Supportive People

To successfully practice the Inquire Within Program, it's imperative you surround yourself with people to support you as you ask questions of yourself and others. This will create a safe environment for your work.

If you choose to hang around people who aren't inquisitive about the world inside and outside themselves, your progress in this program may be stunted or grind to a halt. Those who choose not to question are usually not introspective and for various reasons are threatened by people who do examine their lives.

Exercise Brings Joy and Confidence

Physical exercise is an important part of the Inquire Within Program because moving your body is healthy for your body, mind, and spirit. I can think of ten great reasons to get out there and work your body:

1. You look better when you exercise regularly,
2. You can better manage your weight when you work out,
3. Exercise gives you a sense of confidence and inner strength,
4. The endorphins produced by exercise help you feel calm and peaceful,

5. Regular exercise gives you more control over your life,
6. Working out regularly improves your physical and mental health,
7. Devotion to exercise will teach you to use motivation for other goals,
8. Exercise lowers stress,
9. Exercise helps you solve problems, think clearly, and feel more open to self-questioning, and
10. Exercise is fun!

Before beginning an exercise program, ask your physician if you're medically cleared to work out regularly. Ask her if you should limit the frequency and intensity of your workouts.

Once you have your MD's approval, then you can think about what kind of activity to pursue. Try and recall the last time you exercised and what type of workout you enjoyed. I recommend a program that focuses on your cardio-vascular system.

If you're like many of us , you haven't formally exercised for years and spend much of your adult life in a sedentary position. In that case, the best starting point is to walk a few blocks once a day and gradually increase the distance each week. Keep increasing speed and distance until you feel you're getting a strenuous workout.

Looking back at your earlier years, what sports did you enjoy or always want to try? Perhaps you dreamed about running a marathon. You might join a running club and learn how to train for such an event. Maybe you played basketball as a teenager and long to return to the courts and work on your three-point shot. Maybe you love to dance and you're addicted to "Dancing with the Stars." Don't watch from the sidelines – sign up for dance classes! Your exercise program should be something that's fun and accessible. Yoga, martial arts, spinning classes, and water aerobics offer fun opportunities to renew your body and spirit.

My favorite activity is running, which I've been doing for over thirty years. I enjoy jogging because it's fast and easy for me to put on my running clothes and head out the door. I don't have to wait around for other people and can be alone with my thoughts as I listen to music on my iPod. I hope you'll also find a passion for something that inspires you to move.

Exercise can return your spirit to the days of your youth and innocence, when moving your body was fun. I recommend setting goals each week regarding the frequency and duration of your workout. For example, you may plan to walk one mile per day five days a week and also take a Yoga class once a week to build strength and flexibility. Having fun and experiencing joy are the most essential ingredients.

Once you complete the training outlined in this chapter, you will feel a sense of power, directedness, and optimism. Now you're ready to move on.

NOTES

Chapter 5

Inquire Within Case Studies

In this chapter you'll read about the lives of six people who agreed to share their journey through the Inquire Within Program. Names have been changes to maintain confidentiality. The study includes five women and one man, plus the author's entry. Keep a pen handy, because you may be inspired to form your own questions, but remember not to actually start the Inquire Within Program until you have completed the entire book.

The studies you're about to explore contain excerpts from:
- The Inquire Within Questionnaire, which teaches you how to ask emotional pain questions,
- The Internal Psychotherapist, which shows you how to ask the questions a therapist would ask, and
- If It Were Someone Else and Not You, an exercise that lets you focus on yourself from another person's perspective.

As you'll see, these people courageously faced the emotional pain of sexual molestation, rape, neglect, and child abuse, as well as dealing with the death of a loved one, parenting issues, domestic violence, divorce, living with chronic pain, crises of faith, and being the adult child of an alcoholic.

Their stories depict hurtful experiences, insights about their pain, and solutions to recovery so they can move forward. The insights they uncover validate the notion that we all hold our own answers, and by asking the right questions we can discover our inner truths.

~ ~ ~ ~

Mary B.

Mary B. is a 28-year-old Latina woman who has had difficulty with primary relationships because of the extremely hostile separation and divorce of her parents. As a child, she was constantly put in the middle of her parents' conflicts, where she was overtly and indirectly asked to take sides. She felt her needs were secondary to the adults' feeling, and it was her role to take care of the emotional needs of her parents. She learned from her father that anger is a scary thing and from her mother anger should be suppressed at all times. She had no role models for forming healthy, nurturing relationships.

As an adult, Mary has been in a series of emotionally and physically abusive relationships where she felt trapped, frightened, and alone. Men have questioned her character, spit on her, and hit her in the face. She now recognizes the red flags of danger when she initially meets a man. While Mary has learned not to pursue abusive relationships, she is still searching for a partner and trying to understand her own needs. She works as a news reporter for a large Midwestern city and loves her job.

The Inquire Within Questionnaire

In your opinion, are you unhappy too much of the time?

"Yes"

Do you want to be happier, more often?

"Yes"

What thoughts and feelings surface about your unhappiness?

"In this moment in my life, which is like a rainbow at the end of a powerful tornado, the issue that still makes me unhappy is the desire to have a healthy, long-lasting relationship. I feel I'm ready to have that since I'm now in a space where I continue to work on myself. I love what I do professionally, and I'm probably the most confident I've been in my life. BUT, unhappiness still surrounds the fear of not finding an amazing relationship. I finally believe I deserve it, but I don't know how to explain that. It's like you can be scared of getting what you say you want. What if I get it? Will I know how to keep it? What if I lose it? I still have these questions drenched in fear and unhappiness."

What is the first question you want to ask yourself about your unhappiness?

"Why do I sometimes feel anxious about finding someone?"

What is the answer to this question?

"I feel anxious about finding someone and being in a relationship because I'm scared of being alone or never finding a relationship that will work. Whenever I meet someone, I have to be conscious NOT to rush into a relationship just because I want to be in a relationship, or because at times I am desperate to have a partnership that really works.

I tend to put hope into the connection with him before I actually begin to know him. This is a pattern I'm working hard to change. I just feel like I've had to learn how to have a good relationship on my own because my parents did not provide a healthy example. I've had to figure this out on my own and I'm still trying to understand it."

> BOB'S COMMENTARY: Mary's parents divorced when she was four years old. They fought frequently and loudly. Mary always felt anxious and worked hard to make her mother happy and calm her father. She learned to believe her role in life was to take care of others and ignore her own needs.

What are your follow-up questions and answers about being unhappy?

Do I feel unhappy?

"Not if I deal with it. Unhappiness is sometimes a choice."

What if I get disappointed again?

"I will know how to protect myself. I can always visit my safe space when I'm hurting. I don't want to feel disappointed, but if I do, then I can and will deal with it. I don't need to live in fear of disappointment; this will only serve to make me unhappy."

What happens if I start to feel I can't make myself happy?

"That's when I'll be sure to make an appointment with my therapist and discuss this with someone else. If I don't think I can make me better, then I should feel good about getting outside help. This is my life and I don't want to spend it being unhappy."

> BOB'S COMMENTARY: Like other adult survivors of child abuse and neglect, Mary is intelligent and has superb survival skills. When we focus all

our energy on trying to survive, we don't have the luxury of considering the fact that we can find joy in our own lives. Mary B. is at a point in her life where she sees that possibility.

Assessing whether or not you're unhappy is an exellent first question to ask yourself. The answer will help you begin opening your mind, emotions, and spirit through examining how content you are in the world.

Mary B. might also ask herself: "What happened in my childhood that causes me to feel hopeless about finding a lasting, healthy relationship?"

We gain insight and direction by asking ourselves questions that connect present day unhappiness with events from our childhood. Once we understand why, how, and when the dysfunctional patterns began, we can begin to understand what happened and see the injustice that occurred. Then we can take steps to change our lives.

What are your thoughts and feelings about being emotionally stuck?

"I am not emotionally stuck at this point in my life. I've been emotionally stuck before and it is a miserable place to be. A couple of years ago I dated someone who was clear about not wanting to be in a relationship, but I liked this man so much I was willing to take what I could get. Well I ended up feeling frightened by how much I liked him. This fear caused me to feel confused and lose myself in my need to love and be loved. The fear also caused me to make poor decisions. He was clear about not wanting committed relationship with me. I was overwhelmed with this knowledge and the burning desire to make him want me. I ended up sabatoging the entire relationship by sleeping with his best friend. On some unconcious level I was trying to push his limits in order to terminate this relationship because I was steeped in self-hatred at the time. This is what happens to you when you have a series of relationships where your partners abuse you physically and emotionally.

"I couldn't get over him for a long time because I blew it. It took a long time to forgive myself and move on because I believed no one compared to him. Being emotionally stuck is like being locked into something and you can't move on. Living in the present like this is impossible, so you end up missing out on what's really going on. Getting out of being emotionally stuck can take a long time. Most of the time it lasts longer than you want it to."

Do any of these emotional states apply to you:
Are you fixated on a person or event:

"Yes"

> BOB'S COMMENTARY: Allow yourself to focus on feeling stuck and observe what memories, feelings, and other thoughts come up. What is the first question you would want to ask yourself about being fixated, or emotionally stuck?

Why were you so fixated on that person?

"Because he possessed many of the qualities I look for in a guy, plus the fact that he was sort of emotionally unavailable made me want to win him over even more. I wanted him to validate me, but in the process, I started to fall hard for him. Because I had never been in a healthy, long-lasting relationship, I became fearful of the way he made me feel. He was kind and sweet, even though he continually stated he wasn't interested in a loving relationship. He did put effort in attempting to forge a friendship with me. Once I became sexually intimate with him, my feelings grew and so did my fear. And I knew in the back of my mind that sleeping with his best friend would end whatever relationship we did have. This act dictated the termination of our connection. This was a clear case of self-sabotage! After that I was fixated on the shoulda-woulda-coulda and I couldn't get him out of my head. I dreaded running into him, yet I badly wanted to see him. I compared any men I met to him, because in reality I just wanted another opportunity to not blow a possible great opportunity for a relationship. Later, I also realized I wasn't fixated on the guy, but on the possibility of being with someone. He was the prototype of who I wanted to be with in a loving, mutual, caring relationship."

> BOB'S COMMENTARY: Mary, like many adults who were abused and/or neglected, has low self-esteem and loads of self-loathing. Part of her felt she didn't deserve a healthy relationship, so she unconsciously sabatoged any connection that held a possiblility of closeness. She found someone who would clearly not commit to her, yet she pursued him anyhow. Now, she is beginning to learn the difference between being addicted to someone and being in love.

What are the follow-up questions and answers about being emotionally stuck?

How can I avoid being emotionally stuck?

"I can't hold onto my losses. I have to deal with my emotions while they're fresh; nurture them, and then go on with my life. As I connect with this lesson and understand why certain things that happen are out of my control, I remind myself to learn the life lesson being presented in each case. I need to pay attention to that. I can be obsessive, so I know I need to learn how to move on and not obsesses or dwell over these issues."

Are there other ways I can avoid being emotionally stuck?

"Most of the time I try to become conscious of my intentions, which I can usually do by asking, 'Why am I doing this?' or 'What is it about this person that I like?' or 'Do I even like this person?' Then I can figure out beforehand how I want to respond before I react to events. This helps me be less impulsive. This process is so hard, but when I actually pull it off, it's great because I feel in control of my emotions, actions, and decisions instead of getting lost in being fixated or emotionally stuck on something I can no longer see clearly."

> BOB'S COMMENTARY: Mary might also ask herself: "What are the red flags I should look for when I first become interested in a man?" A huge red flag is a person who's charming, but emotionally unavailable.
>
> Mary could then ask, "Why am I attracted to men who are not open to having a relationship and why does that cause me to want them to desire me even more?
>
> She might also ask, "Are these men similar to my father? If so, why am I attracted to them?"

The Internal Psychotherapist

Imagine you're in a therapist's office and think about the questions she has for you. What is the first question she might ask?

How are you doing today and is anything bothering you?

"I'm doing good. Work is going well."

Write down your unhappy emotional state here:

"Sometimes I'm concerned I won't find a lasting and healthy relationship."

Ask yourself: What happened to cause this emotional state?

"I know that I've had abusive relationships in the past and I don't have a positive image from either of my parents regarding what a healthy relationship looks like. This makes me fearful that I will never discover this kind of closeness with another person."

> BOB'S COMMENTARY: Mary B. tended to choose abusive partners because she felt her role in a relationship was to take care of and heal her emotionally wounded lovers. The men she chose had characteristics of her father. Her father would frequently cry to her about his troubles and she learned to believe it was her job to take care of him. Below, she pinpoints other reasons for choosing abusive partners.

Ask yourself – Why did this happen?

"I have no idea why this happened, especially since I had no control over my parent's relationship or their ways of relating to the world. I know that having to find balance between my unhappy, divorced parents made me insecure and a people pleaser. The need to obtain approval made me an easy target for predators and abusers. I had to work hard on improving my self-esteem and to learn to love myself. I don't want to fall back into my familiar patterns that have led to broken and disturbing relationships."

> BOB'S COMMENTARY: The third step in the Internal Therapist section is to ask leading questions, such as...
> Why do I feel this way?
> How did this happen?
> How have I dealt with it in the past?
> How would I like to deal with it in the future?
> What do I believe in?

Can you think of other leading questions? Write them down for later, or answer them now.

Is there something I need to forgive myself for?

"Yes! Even though I am responsible for my actions, it's important to forgive myself, especially when something is not my fault, such as my parent's hostile divorce and hateful relationship."

What if I enter another bad relationship?

"I will be better prepared to deal with it, because now I'm aware of how this all works. This knowledge helps keep me from living in fear of a bad relationship, because now I have faith that no matter what happens, I'll be all right."

Is fear involved in how you're feeling? If so, what are you afraid of and are you afraid of allowing the fear to take the wheel and steer?

"I'm afraid of not finding someone or not having a healthy relationship. In unguarded moments I can allow the fear to take over, which causes me to lose my logical thinking and act purely on emotional impulse. This tends to make the situation more dire."

Do I now realize how difficult life has been for me?

"Yes, I do recognize how difficult life had been for me. I always try to keep that in mind. I find it easy to empathize with my friends and loved ones, but difficult to feel empathy for myself."

Addressing painful childhood memories.

What is the most painful memory?

"Since my parents often fought with one another, my most painful childhood memories involve wondering whether their love for me was stonger than their hatered for each other. These experiences with my parents made me uncomfortable expressing any emotions with them or anyone else. Therefore, during most of my life I hid my true feelings from significant others."

BOB'S COMMENTARY: What other questions could Mary ask herself?

~ ~ ~ ~

Melinda M.

Melinda M. is a 32-year-old Puerto Rican woman with a 15-year-old daughter. Melinda has suffered from an eating disorder for years. Her mother is an alcoholic and her father suddenly abandoned the family when she was five. She is a performance artist who acts and sings in New York City where she lives. She was in a long-term relationship with a man before she ended it because she felt he wasn't emotionally or financially supportive. Her struggles with being from an alcoholic family are highlighted here.

The Inquire Within Questionnaire

Emotional Pain Question:

What obstacles in my childhood do I need to overcome in order to move forward as an adult?

"Obstacles from my youth include dealing with peers. This was a big issue because I didn't really feel I was included in anything. I didn't feel whole. I didn't feel accepted at home and that leaves me feeling bad about living with an alcoholic mother and growing up without a father."

BOB'S COMMENTARY: Adult children of alcoholics do have difficulty forming healthy relationships. The rules in their families are hard fast and ridged, yet subject to change without notice. This dynamic creates a sense of anxiety that has plagued Melinda throughout her adult life. Notice how she returns to the same themes.

"My poor economic status was a problem for me, because I couldn't afford the brand name clothes my peers wore. Not having these material items made me feel I didn't fit in because discussion about these clothes played a huge role while I was going to high school. I constantly looked for ways to feel accepted. If I had money or clothes, I felt I would have been valued more by my peers. Everybody had the Nikes, Cross Colours and Jabos, but not me. This reinforced the feeling that I didn't fit in. I felt better about fitting in when I played sports and got good grades, but overall, I felt I was much different from these kids. The feeling of being an outcast affected my self-esteem and self-image."

Other questions Melinda could ask herself:

Why was it important for me to fit in?

What price did I pay by not fitting in?

> BOB'S COMMENTARY: If you find yourself feeling deprived of love, connections, financial security, or compassion, it's helpful to ask yourself about the price you've paid for being in this position. The answer may help you open up to feelings of loss and help you grieve over the pain you've experienced.

"I felt part of my family as a whole. I'm the oldest grandchild. In my own primary family (mother and brother), I felt I was part of that, but I always kept my distance because I never believed I could make my mother happy. Nothing I did pleased her. If I got good grades she told me I was supposed to get good grades. Yes, I was playing sports, but she said, 'You better be home on time.' My birthday was frequently overlooked. I feel I have disregarded myself because of all of this. I sometimes feel uncomfortable when attention isn't focused on me, but on the flip side, I want to be noticed. This creates a conflict. I feel unsettled sometimes. I know I want to be recognized for my singing, but I'm not sure if I should want this. I sometimes think wanting to be recognized is conceited, or it's immodest to purposely bring attention to myself. I wonder if I'm being wholesome and feel guilty for wanting this goal.

"Yet, it doesn't feel good to play small/immodest/invisible much of the time. I know as a singer, I need to have my stuff out there. I want to find a balance, but I don't know how. This came from my childhood because I never felt I was wanted or stood out. I felt wanted in church choir while my mother played the piano, and I knew she was proud of my singing in church. Music was her love and she should have been proud for me to do anything musical in church, because my singing made folks happy. This was my love, but she didn't recognize it. She never told me I was great or encouraged me to pursue my dreams of being a singer. I never got the talk about that from her. I wasn't recognized for my talents without qualifiers ('You're good, but you need to work to improve'), or separate from my mom's activities."

Other questions Melinda could ask herself:

How can I learn to resolve the conflict between wanting to be noticed and feeling like I want to disappear?

> BOB'S COMMENTARY: Defining her dilemma puts Melinda on the road to solving this problem. She realizes her need to be invisible is based on fear, while the desire to be acknowledged is derived from her need to be loved. If you find yourself asking a question and having a long answer, I recommend you stop and return to the previous material. Look for conflicts and attempt to define them as a question. This will help you clarify and create other self-questions.

"I had to constantly walk on egg shells. This taught me to be a mouse and not make a sound; to be invisible. This is in contrast to putting me out there and being real visible. Ultimately, I was striving for peace in my household, but if my mother was too quiet or snappy, that was a bad omen and a signal she might erupt in anger at any moment. She would yell and scream at me for reasons I couldn't understand. She would call me fat and manipulative. I needed to be quiet and invisible to prevent this from happening. Now, I get triggered when people close to me are quiet. I wonder if I'm doing something wrong that will cause them to explode. I try to break the silence to ensure everything is okay. I still get triggered by my mother, even though she has been in recovery for years. I'm afraid to talk to her about all this for fear she won't listen or will blame me for her actions.

"I don't withhold myself from my mother, because I don't feel that is in my best interests. Even now she can be toxic, but I don't want to abandon her. I'm afraid to talk about this; I don't want her to have any more pain, and she's been through so much. I don't think she's wise enough to realize this feeling of mine is from the past, not the present or the future. I believe she will take it personally in the present. I'm afraid she will dismiss my feelings once again."

Other questions Melinda could ask herself:

Why am I fearful of my mother's reactions – feeling angry, wanting her approval, and being protective of her feelings all at the same time?

BOB'S COMMENTARY: This is another type of conflict we can turn into a question by reading and rereading our stories. Melinda's opposing feelings toward her mother are common for adults who've been abused and neglected. The work here is to examine each of these dynamics one at a time, and then bring them together.

Melinda now understands that she views the world the same way she perceives her mother. She also learns it's impossible to hold all three of these feelings at the same time. No wonder she feels stuck and confused at times!

Another question might be:

Why do I have the need to protect my mother from feeling bad, even when I know her actions have hurt me and I have the right to confront her?

"If I could have this conversation with my mother, I might improve the contentious relationship. I don't feel I'm free. At times I'm not sure if a belief is mine or influenced by someone else. I wonder if it's me when I go through experiences like I did with my ex-boyfriend who wasn't emotionally or financially available. I wonder if it's me when I go through experiences and end up knowledgeable about the situation. I don't feel like this is acceptable because I am 32 years old and I should be more sure about myself.

"I feel angry at myself because I can't be sure if my feelings are my own, or influenced by someone else. I feel like time is passing and I should be able to make up my mind about things. I don't think I'm worthy of giving myself permission to be myself. I feel like I'm constantly walking on eggshells as I had to when I lived with my volatile, alcoholic mother. My mother would yell at me for no reason; I never knew when she would yell or hit me. I often took the blame for my younger brother's infractions. If he didn't clean his room, I would tell my mom it was my fault and I would be punished."

Other questions Melinda could ask herself:

Why am I unsure if my feelings are my own or influenced by someone else?

BOB'S COMMENTARY: This question may lead to the discovery that because Melinda took so much responsibility for her mother's feelings, she hasn't learned to separate what feelings are actually hers, versus what feelings come from someone else. People who grew up in alcoholic families often have boundary issues. Melinda learned early in life that her role was to sacrifice her own needs in order to take care of and rescue other family members.

"If my mother was very quiet, then I knew to be on guard, because a firestorm might come at any moment. To this day I am uncomfortable with silence.

"She also instilled in me that if I start something, I need to finish it. That has positive and negative effects. The positive is that when I start something, I do finish it. The downside is that I'm afraid to start things because I am afraid I won't finish.

"I do avoid things I'm fearful of. I'm afraid to confront my mother about how she treated me. I don't want to hurt her feelings, and at times I get confused about her feelings and my own feelings.

"I'm used to not putting expectations on things. I recently learned it's okay to place expectations on my daughter. I told her I expect her to get good grades and hang around with good kids. I'm trying to learn when it's appropriate to have expectations of others and when it isn't. I felt mature at my daughter's school. I told her she needed to improve her grades, and I told the teachers I had these expectations. I guess I didn't feel I had the right to do this before."

Other questions Melinda could ask:
What kind of mother do I want to be?
Is it important to set limits for my daughter?
If so, how can I best accomplish that?

What are the best discipline methods?

What gets stirred up in me if my daughter doesn't listen to me or show me respect?

> BOB'S COMMENTARY: Questions about parenting help you assess how well you're functioning in that role. Melinda finds herself ill-equipped to raise her own daughter because she did not have a healthy role model from her parents. However, her intelligence and willingness to look at her own behavior will help her improve her parenting skills.

"My expectations of my friends have been that they are to come through for me, but often that hasn't been the case. I have lots of expectations for myself. I'm used to people not coming through for me, but I'm afraid of not coming through for myself. I need to find courage and let go of control if I want to pursue my goals of being a dancer and performer.

"I need to be flexible about my expectations. The expectations my mother had for me were rigid. She had high expectations, but never praised me for anything. She never went to my sporting events or other activities. This rigidity is one reason I still walk on eggshells. My mother would tell me I was too fat and when I got good grades she would say, "You better get good grades!" There was never praise or the sense of unconditional love."

Other questions Melinda could ask herself:

How did my mother's rigidity affect me?

> BOB'S COMMENTARY: This is a good question, and the answers will help Melinda understand why she may be rigid and inflexible in certain areas. The answers will help her discover different behaviors and attitudes, making her more tolerant, flexible, and open to life.

"I need to let go of my perceived outcome for experiences. Rigidity has kept the expectations without flexibility or wiggle room.

"My psychology teacher in college asked me if either of my parents was an alcoholic because I would not deviate from the straight line. This insight opened up a whole new world for me.

"I want to be myself, without this force behind me. I had to force others to see who I am: how I dress, how I wear my hair, what kind of music I listen to.

"My goal is to not walk on egg shells anymore. I've had to bulldoze through all this stuff. Acting like a human bulldozer is a way of protecting myself – or maybe I was more like a tank, because I use this attitude to protect myself and I need armor to keep anyone from stopping me from moving forward. The armor comes with an attitude; sometimes I block you out, and other times I tell myself I don't care what others think of me. This happens in auditions. In grade school, I was one of the only children of color, and the other kids made fun of me. They would make fun of my clothes because I didn't have the expensive things others wore. I pushed myself to do well academically and athletically. When I realized nothing I could do would change their minds, I developed an attitude of F---K you. The kids must have thought I was crazy. My choice was to be fearful and timid or develop a defiant attitude that came from a place of deep hurt.

"The process works like this: I become terrified when I'm on a job interview or an audition, and then I get angry and tell myself I can accomplish whatever I am faced with. I go into a cocoon and sometimes I'm not aware of what I am doing. I am fearful of being judged, but I have to be judged if I'm going to be an actress.

"I remember when I was a little kid I would sing in the kitchen all by myself. I would sing harmonies when no one was home. I felt like I was me, letting it go. I'm supposed to be aware of myself when

I'm performing, but often times I am not present. I go to this other place, and sometimes when I sing I am not present or aware of what I'm doing. I sing on auto pilot, and despite not being present I get great feedback from others. I think the fear of being judged pushes me out of the present. I would like to be more aware. Like many things in my life, I am in conflict with this. I can see both sides of all issues. I don't want to change this disassociating while performing because when it happens I don't judge myself or worry – there is no inner chatter. I feel I sing better when I'm not present.

"When I was with my boyfriend in my early 20s, I had the experience of not being present. This was the first time I realized I was not emotionally present. This is in contrast to my time in church, where I felt like I was part of everyone. My singing belonged to the whole church experience and I wasn't separate and alone."

> BOB'S COMMENTARY: The honest and thought-provoking work Melinda did here resulted in a meeting with her mother. In this meeting, Melinda's mom took responsibility for demanding too much from her daughter. She also admitted that drinking caused her to be unreasonable, mean, and too much of a perfectionist. Her mother shared how much her divorce from Melinda's father devastated her. Melinda was surprised and gratified by how forthright her mother was in this meeting. Many tears were shed and they are on the way to healing their relationship and finding love and trust.

What other questions would you like to see Melinda ask herself? Will these questions work for you?

~ ~ ~ ~

Aida C.

Aida C. is a thirty-one-year-old woman whose father was African-American and mother was Columbian. She has three children and lives in Chicago. As a child she was neglected, beaten, and sexually assaulted. She was a gang member and has witnessed many incidents of violence. Aida is presently going to law school and plans to finish this spring. She is working hard to resolve trust issues in her life and is fiercely protective of children because of the abuse she suffered as a kid. Although being alone without a partner feels safe for her, she is presently exploring a primary relationship. She is searching to discover what a healthy relationship is.

Do you have an internal safe place, and what is it like?

"My first response to 'Do I have a safe space to go to' is 'Hell No!' When something is coming at me so hard I have to put myself in a box, I turn to prayer, asking God for strength. I haven't been able to picture a safe place inside me.

"Praying is something I do for myself. I begin to pray when I'm upset, angry, or hurt and I see red. When I'm to myself in my own world, sometimes prayer works and other times it doesn't."

Other questions AIDA might ask herself:

Why is it difficult for me to create an internal safe space?

BOB'S COMMENTARY: This question may help Aida realize that if she allows herself to relax, the quiet time will trigger a fearful response based on the multiple traumas in her past. In other words, letting down her guard makes her feel vulnerable to potential danger. This is the opposite of the soothing effects this exercise should produce. The answers to this question may help Aida find gradual steps to creating a safe space inside.

What is your calming music playlist and how does it affect you?

"Immortal Technique, Leaving the Past and You Never Know,

"A Moment for Life by Nicki Minaj,

"Three Little Birds by Bob Marley,

"We want Freedom by Dead Prez,

"How I Got Over by The Roots,

"Most of songs by Tupac – especially Death Around the Corner and the Thuglife CD.

"This music brings up my childhood because I lived the street life he and Biggy sing about. I both reminisce and look at how far I've come from living that life style. Being a parent, I cannot be part of that anymore – I can't be a criminal. The consequences are too severe. I can listen to this music today and release some of the pain I felt back then. I'm having it replay in my head, but I'm not acting it out, so it calms me down. Music is my place of peace and freedom. I need to have it with me at all times.

"Most of the music I listen to is from males. Not much is feminine. I relate to their struggles. When I'm missing my mother who died from cancer when I was a little girl, I listen to Watermark by Enya. That is what I was listening to when she died. I listen to all the old Santana stuff, because it reminds me of when my mother was alive and very much in her heroin addiction. The memories are comforting or disturbing, depending on what comes up. Being that I lost my mother at a young age, I gravitate toward the music she found moving and electric. I live my life for music. I seem to relate to men more than women when it comes to musical selections. Perhaps that's because my childhood and early adulthood was plagued by violence. I think society has it wrong when they say men tend to use violence as a first response. Women also play this out. Women have the potential to do the crazier things. I know. I've seen it."

Other questions AIDA could ask herself:

Why do women have the potential to act out more than men?

> BOB'S COMMENTARY: The answer to this may be that women in our society are more powerless than men and are sometimes viewed as prey. Men receive both subtle and overt permission to dominate women, and this power/control frequently leads to violence against women. The emotional pain perpetrated against women sometimes causes them to become violent themselves as a way to survive. Aida's violence is learned behavior where survival is the name of the game. She is working to determine the roots of her anger. Perhaps it derives from the hurt she expresses in response to the next questions.

How do I express my feelings?

"I'm capable of being violent toward others. If I'm able to cuss people out, I can to temporarily release my pain. I feel this prevents me from actually hitting someone. In my life I wasn't allowed to show weakness. I learned this value from the streets and in jail. If you show weakness you'll be taken advantage of – big time.

"Women are more vicious to each other. When I was locked up, I kept my mouth shut. I learned quickly this was the best way to survive the prison system. My childhood, where I had to constantly be on guard for attack, taught me how to live in the jail. My childhood taught me how to be institutionalized. The times I got into trouble with my mother, the more I cried, the more I got whooped. I learned to keep me feelings to myself in order to not be beaten to death."

Other questions AIDA could ask herself:

How did being incarcerated affect my life?
How did it change me?
What does it mean to be institutionalized?

> BOB'S COMMENTARY: Being imprisoned can have a profound effect on a person's life. You're told what to do and when to do it. You have meals prepared for you (granted, most of these meals are tasteless) and a roof over your head. You learn to be robotic and go along with the program. You learn to be even more distrustful of others and to repress all your anger and sadness. If you do express negative feelings, you'll be penalized by more time to serve or isolation. So then the question becomes, "How do I emotionally recover from being imprisoned? This question should help Aida identify her feelings and begin healing from this pain,"

"I do the same thing with my kids. 'What the hell are you crying about?' I realize I'm teaching these habits to my children as well, because I don't want them to fall victim to anybody. I know what can happen. I feel telling them not to cry or show vulnerability will get them ready to deal with this hard-ass world when they grow up. If I'm not here, who's going to teach them? I do have the ability to separate out when my kids need to cry because they got their feelings hurt versus being tearful because they got in trouble with me. I can separate this out for them, but I'm still learning how to do it for myself.

"I have many physical symptoms: headaches, stomach aches, neck aches, back pain, fatigue, and eating too much or too little. This is based on 'you hurt me, so now I'll hurt myself.' I won't eat. If a guy is hurting me I lose my appetite. If the world is coming at me – no money, no foreseeable job, I eat too much. This is soothing at the moment and also causes me to gain weight, which makes me bigger and more threatening. Therefore, I have less to fear if someone tries to harm me physically or mentally. I'm already strong, and the bigger I am, the stronger I am.

"School makes me unhappy and angry. My law school doesn't go out of the way to help me. It's a real struggle for me. They promised me all this help they never delivered. Outside of school, being alone makes me unhappy – I have no adult family for support. I have been unhappy my whole life. I ask for happiness when I pray. Sometimes I yell out for it. I know why people kill themselves. I know why people do dope. I know why people kill. What are we going to do to feel peace?"

Other questions AIDA could ask herself:

How can I calm and soothe myself without being self-destructive?

> BOB'S COMMENTARY: This is a great question for those of us who have a history of escaping painful feelings through drug addiction, alcoholism, or any other unhealthy distraction. Possibly the answer is "I don't know." Then perhaps the next question can be "How do I find ways to calm and soothe myself without being self-destructive?" This may involve going to therapy, attending a self-help group, or reading more about this topic.

"I want my children to be happy. I hope I don't interfere with their happiness. I don't know what it was like to be an innocent child. I was selling dope at my daughter's age of nine. I never got a chance to play as a kid. Because of that I am not patient when my kids act silly and create an imaginary world. I don't get this. I never experienced this."

Other questions AIDA could ask herself:

What did I miss by not having a normal childhood?

> BOB'S COMMENTARY: This is a good question for many people, because the answers will help us understand what we missed and how that void affects us in the present moment. It may also lead to grief about our lost childhood innocence and the fact that we never felt safe and protected.

"I'm also conscious that I am finally in a good relationship with a man, but I worry that I will sabotage it because deep down inside I don't believe I deserve to be loved. If I prepare myself for being hurt, I believe I will be hurt less when I am betrayed."

> BOB'S COMMENTARY: The next section displays what can happen when we ask the right questions. I don't believe you will ask a particular question if you aren't prepared to deal with the answer. Yes, the answer can be devastating and cause an overwhelming emotional response, such as tears coming up from your guts. But in the long term you'll feel more secure and happier because you faced your own truth.

What questions would you like to ask about your unhappiness?

"Why am I unhappy? When I was a child my innocence was taken from me. Because of that I will never be able to experience an actual orgasm. I was raped by many men, beginning when I was five or six years old. I never told anyone about this and this is the first time I have actually written it down. I have to spend my whole life pretending to have an orgasm, to fake being in ecstasy.

"I am afraid to tell my partner I can't fully enjoy making love because of what happened to me during my childhood. I remember being molested and raped by a number of people. My mother was never around because she was strung out on heroin. She would have men in the neighborhood watch me while she was out. I wonder what she was thinking. I would go random places with her and she would leave me with strange men while she got high. I could never sleep then. I was afraid to close my eyes, and I have problems sleeping to this day. I learned to sleep with weapons as a little girl in order to protect myself from the perpetrators who would find their way to me. I remember bringing a butter knife to bed with me.

"At the end of the day, I am messed up and programmed to please others. Every relationship I have ever had, I've been the one to please. At times it seemed others tried to please me too, but it just didn't feel right.

"I don't remember how old I was when the molestation and rapes began, but I was very little. I do recall a situation with a guy who looked so pitiful. He was sad, always walking around the housing projects where I lived. He was well-dressed, but easy prey. I remember saying to myself that maybe I should have sex with him and take his money. I was about eight years old. This is screwed up. I must have developed this mentality from being abused and molested. It was like prostitution was implanted in my brain.

"Perhaps this came from witnessing my mother having sex with a man right in front of me. Again, I believe I was seven or eight and my mother and this dude were going at it right in front of me like I wasn't even there. I remember being in a crib. I don't know if it was my dad or some other guy. I didn't know who it was. This scene was shocking and without any boundaries.

"Drugs were a big part of my community. They were used to make money and make them forget their pain.

"My mother used to take me to other folk's houses where she had sex, and she made no effort to shield me from their raucous activity. I don't know what she was thinking, but I am angry now, because this led me to have a fearful, guarded attitude about sex and sexuality. I am so ashamed that this happened and don't think any man can really understand what happened to me.

"I rarely allow my kids to spend the night with anyone. I need to be 100 percent certain my kids will be safe. I don't ever want them to go through what happened to me.

"Sometimes I wonder what happened with my father. I know he was from the streets – a drug dealer and perhaps a murderer. He was messed up. Why couldn't my dad treat my mother right so she didn't have to sleep with men to get money for drugs? Was my mother strung out on dope because my father was abusing her in some fashion? When I think about all this, I wonder who triggered whom to do what. My father was a controlling man and I know he controlled all his women, but who was there to protect me? Sometimes my mom would leave me at school until the police would come to take me to a shelter because she forgot to pick me up. What kind of crap is that? This still sits with me. I wish I could remember how old I was.

"Then through all that, I had to act like a happy child, like things were all right. I remember in pre-school the boys pulling down my pants and placing a stick in my vagina. Where the hell were the teachers? I was victimized throughout my life and no one was there to protect me. I felt like I was less than invisible."

Other questions AIDA could ask herself:

What was it like recounting my abuse story for the first time?

> BOB'S COMMENTARY: Telling your story to yourself or another person for the first time is a major event, because you no longer have to

stuff all this angst deep inside. In Aida's case, repressing this trauma was necessary and effective during her childhood. It helped her survive during the period in her life when she couldn't afford to dwell on, or try to understand, why all these terrible things were happening to her. However, continued repression of these feelings may lead to physical illness and lead her to continue the same self-destructive patterns. Now she has the possibility of looking at them with the assistance of a therapist, while using Inquire Within to supplement working through all this horror.

"People say I have trust issues. No kidding! And why would I be able to trust? The combination of being emotionally and physically violated while no one paid attention to what was happening to me was hurtful and confusing.

"I am having a difficult time because programs that are supposed to be helping me threaten to cut me off if I don't have a job. I'm looking for work, attending law school, and raising two young children. It seems no one is giving me a break, but I don't want to go into victim mode either.

"I do have an interview scheduled for next week and I'm optimistic about landing this executive assistant position. It is hard out there where jobs are very difficult to find, but I'm hopeful that I will find one.

"I am seeking a sense of community I believe I am finding in Islam. I need to learn to pray effectively. I have faith and want to expand it."

How is faith going to help me?

"Religion has always been phony for me in the past, but my relationship with God as a Muslim is getting deeper. If I don't follow the steps I'm supposed to take, that is up to me. This is different from Christianity where so much of what we learn is derived from guilt. If I don't do as I'm told, I will be punished and be letting God down. The sisterhood from my Muslim community brings me peace and joy that is different from Christianity, which seems so phony.

"I feel no pressure in this community and I get so emotional because of the beauty of the religion and the connection of the people. This seems like home to me and I am one who has never felt safe or had a protected space.

"My faith gives me strength, clarity, wisdom, understanding, and patience. I am not going to ask God for a job or money. I will ask God if He will guide me to the places I need to go to obtain a job."

How do I know what a good relationship is?

"I'm trying to find peace within myself, but I am so tired of struggling. For the first time in my life I am in a healthy relationship with a man. He recently moved in with me after a long-term, long-distance relationship. I'm not sure what to expect because all my relationships in the past have been filled with emotional and physical violence. I always expected that a man would physically hurt me. This is no longer acceptable to me.

"I am afraid of losing him. I know I have abandonment issues because no one has ever been there for me. I know he's committed to me, but I don't fully trust his words because of the track record I've had in my life. My parents abused and abandoned me. I have had friends who have died violent deaths and were suddenly gone. I always have my guard up and would someday like to lower it.

"I am afraid to let him know about my past. What man wants to hear that I was raped, molested, beaten and abandoned? I have not shared my past with anyone. I am afraid that he will feel that I have too much baggage and then he will leave. But, hell he has a lot of baggage too and I am able to tolerate that. This relationship is so difficult and I am not sure the needs I have are okay to have.

"I was always taught that men desire my body and that's one asset I can utilize. If I really want my man to stay, I have to give him sex. However, I don't enjoy sex because I can never relax. I'm always focused on the possibility of something horrible happening. Men in my life have been so volatile and unpredictable.

"When I am ready to share these deep things with him, he starts to get angry like he doesn't want to hear what I want to say. I want to open up, but I don't want to be slammed during the process.

"There are so many good things about this relationship. He said he was moving out here to be with me. I don't think anyone has said anything like this to me before. I want to learn how to be vulnerable, but I don't know how. It is a challenge, and I think it would be best to not let my memories interfere with what is happening in the present.

"Sleeping is a problem for me because of the trauma I've had in my life. In some of my relationships, the first thing that happened when I woke up was that I got beaten up. I don't think my current boyfriend will do this, but I still worry he will become violent although he doesn't seem to have any of the signs.

"I witnessed my mother being beaten continually by my father. I remember witnessing him and my mother having sex. These memories begin when I was a baby. I wonder if my mother was always having sex with my father or was it another man. I often wonder if my mother was a prostitute. There were no boundaries in my young life and I don't know appropriate boundaries now."

Other questions AIDA could ask herself:

How did witnessing my parents having sex affect me?

> BOB'S COMMENTARY: This is an important question to ask because it speaks to the fact that appropriate boundaries in her family were non-existent. She could ask later, "How did this lack of boundaries affect my relationships with others?" Thus far, Aida has learned that the lack of boundaries in childhood caused her to be fearful and distrustful of others, while at the same time created a powerful need to be loved and accepted.

"My father used to provide the heroin for my mother. When she took me to someone's house, she didn't make sure that house was safe. She would often leave me with these strangers and I would be molested or beaten. It didn't feel safe to ask these strangers where my mother was. She would just disappear and not tell me where she was going. It wasn't safe to show any fear or weakness – you had to be hard. I couldn't cry and ask these people for anything. I never knew the outcome of any of these visits. I don't remember her coming back to get me, or anything else, besides being in a smoked out house with psychedelic music in the background.

"If my mother was still alive I would probably not allow my kids around her and I certainly would have a lot of questions for her. My mother was a large woman who weighed over 300 pounds. She got real sick with cancer when I was only nine years old and I remember being her primary caretaker. I used to bathe her and provide every other service.

"If my boyfriend comes up behind me in the kitchen, I often jump because of all the abuse that occurred in my life. I'm afraid to tell him why I do this, but I don't think he wants to know. I always say that he doesn't really know me, and he says we can deal with this stuff later. He doesn't know how much of a risk I'm taking to even consider telling him about my past. But, I don't know how to approach him. I don't know how to tell him that I really want him to listen to me. I am taking a risk for me and my kids. This is huge.

"He is taking a risk too because of his experiences in life. He had issues at being a victim of violence and abandonment as well. His story may not be as dramatic and traumatic as mine, but I want him to know that I am not his ex and he is not my father or other ex-boyfriend.

"I don't know how I would start that conversation, "I jump when you suddenly approach because...." I'm afraid he will think something is very wrong with me. I don't want to get too relaxed, but I don't want to be so guarded with him either. I'm not sure how to be. This is all so new for me."

> BOB'S COMMENTARY: I'm amazed Aida is still alive, much less trying to finish law school, get a job, and create a healthy intimate relationship. The abuse she suffered caused her to feel she doesn't deserve anything worthwhile in her life. She has to fight against the notion that she will be betrayed, because betrayal is a huge part of her experience. The Inquire Within Program taught her the value of physical and emotional boundaries her parents didn't provide for her. In this gut-wrenching story, she was able to face her sexual molestation for the first time. Experiencing this angst brought her forward one step.

What other questions Aida might ask herself? Would these questions apply to you?

~ ~ ~ ~

Jim G.

Jim G. is a 53-year-old Caucasian man who was been married for 30 years. He has two grown adult children: a boy and a girl. Two years ago his wife was killed while she and Jim were crossing a quiet street. Suddenly, a car sped down the street and hit them, killing her and injuring him. The driver was never caught. Jim has been grieving for his wife ever since, and he frequently feels lost and alone. He's still picking up the pieces, trying to figure out what's possible for him at this stage in his life. He isn't sure he will ever again find joy in his life. He misses his wife and doesn't believe he can find a similar relationship; she was the love of his life. However, he wants to keep an open mind and realizes he can be his own worst enemy. He can be overly self-critical and judgmental of his actions and thoughts. Jim hopes the Inquire Within Program can help him understand his loss and process his grief.

The Inquire Within Questionnaire

What thoughts and feelings come up for you around unhappiness?

> "I feel loss and a sense that the best part of my life is over. I often experience feelings of inadequacy, failure, and unworthiness. I have a desire for security, even though no security is truly available. I'm sometimes preoccupied with the feeling that I have let somebody down and I need to be perfect."

Other questions Jim could ask himself:

Why am I so preoccupied with the feeling that I let someone down?

BOB'S COMMENTARY: This question could help Jim understand that this feeling is a symptom of post traumatic stress disorder that began the day his wife was killed. He can also look back into his childhood and try to understand how having a physically absent father and an emotionally unavailable mother contributed to his present feelings.

"My wife's death has been very difficult to deal with, and I frequently feel lost and alone. I'm picking up the pieces – trying to figure out what's possible at this stage in my life. At times I feel like I'm going through the motions: going to work, socializing a little, and trying to guide my adult kids."

BOB'S COMMENTARY: Jim's loss of his wife was extremely traumatic. He also feels lost because he's still working on the effects of never knowing his father and having a mother he felt was uncaring. While he doesn't seem to find any happiness in his work here, he does face his grief in a direct and profound way. A loss of this magnitude may take a long time to recover from. In Jim's case, recovery may mean simply experiencing the sun shining on his face one day.

Do any of these emotional states apply to you?

Depressed:

"If I allow myself to indulge in this."

Anxious:

"I need constant training to avoid anxiety."

Hopeless:

"The fear that this is my true self."

Other questions Jim could ask himself:

Why do I try to avoid anxiety and does the avoidance help me?

> BOB'S COMMENTARY: This question will help Jim assess his present coping skills. At times, avoiding anxiety by healthy distraction such as exercise, going to a movie, or talking with friends is helpful. Avoiding the thoughts that create anxiety are necessary for survival during the early periond after a loss. However, this avoidance can become dysfunctional. At some point we need to look at what's causing the anxiety and then make attempts to transform those negative thoughts into hopeful ones.

What are the first questions you want to ask yourself about your unhappiness:

What makes me unhappy?

What is happiness anyway?"

"I think happiness is connected to the ego. We all prefer happy, but we need to realize that happiness and sadness are linked together and you can't have one without the other. If I love, I will ultimately grieve. If I am happy, I will eventually be sad if the source of my happiness changes. I prefer to observe both happiness and sadness from a place of non-judgment. I think the answer to unhappiness is acceptance. If I can change the situation, then I should do so. If I cannot, then I must accept unhappiness as a place where I am at right now. Once I observe and isolate the pain and realize it isn't who I am, then I can then let it go.

"Perhaps peace is the true sensation to search for. Whether happy or unhappy, I can be at peace. How can I ever truly be happy? I've lived with melancholy since the day my wife was taken from me. The best I can be right now is to feel sad in a happy (comfortable) way. Once I accepted there was nothing I could do to change my situation, I began to see new insights into dealing with my condition."

Other questions Jim might ask himself:

What does acceptance mean?

> BOB'S COMMENTARY: The answers to this question can help Jim clarify the concept of acceptance by asking other things, such as: Does acceptance mean we no longer think about what's troubling us – that we develop amnesia? Is this what we desire? Is acceptance a permanent emotion and mindset? Or is acceptance a state we reach that includes understanding, but moves in and out of our psyche? Acceptance doen't come with a Hollywood movie ending where the sun sets and all is beautiful forever. We each need to discover our definiton for acceptance in order to move forward.

Do you feel emotionally stuck?

"We all become emotionally stuck at times, especially after a major loss like mine. Losing my partner was devastating and continues to be overwhelming at times. There is a time of limbo afterwards that encourages this stuckness. Grief counseling is vital in offering options to work through these feelings. Being in limbo is a state of not knowing where you want to go with the important aspects of your life. Do I want to move? Should I get into a relationship? Should I change jobs? These questions come up frequently, with no solid answers. The limbo will last longer than the stuckness. I need to be aware of this. Sometimes you have to mark the passing of time for family members and friends who need help with the same grief you're going through."

Do any of these emotional states apply to you: feeling disconnected from others, feeling bored much of the time, or fixated on a person or event?

"Yes, I do experience all of these states."

What is the first question you want to ask about being emotionally stuck?

"Why am I emotionally stuck?

What is the answer?

"My mind fixates on the accident that killed my wife. I relive the event over and over, imagining the gory details even though I was unconscious at the time and have no memory of the event. I have to concentrate on knowing this is a thought, just like any other thought, and I don't need to beat myself up about this."

What are the follow-up questions and answers about being emotionally stuck?

How long will I be stuck in limbo?

"As long as needed or as long as I allow myself to be stuck."

What will come next?

"It's best not to think of the future too much, because this is just as daunting as being stuck. I find it's best to stay in the present moment and have less specific goals that are easy to arrive at. This causes less stress than fixating on the future."

Other questions Jim could ask himself:

Will I ever feel different about my loss, or will the tragedy of losing my wife keep me feeling sad forever?

> BOB'S COMMENTARY: Jim now feels over-whelmed by the pain of abruptly losing his wife. This probing question may bring comfort to Jim, and to others who are experiencing deep grief as they see a glimmer of hope in the future.

What if It Were Someone Else and Not You Exercise

What events have had the greatest impact on this person's life?

"His birth and the circumstances of his birth, including the fact that he never met his father.

"Marriage and moving to the west coast to begin the grand adventure.

"The birth of his children – totally life changing events.

"The accidental death of his wife, shattering the magic; the moment he started gaining consciousness and realizing something was wrong, but was still too disoriented to understand what happened. To be told he was picked off the ground and his wife didn't survive. The complete and utter realization of his life in shattered pieces."

Did you learn anything new about yourself from completing this exercise?

"I realized how vulnerable I still am. I carefully thought about all these questions before answering them. Doing so wasn't easy. Completing this case study was depressing, because it emphasized my situation. In the present moment I am free of pain, at least for a while. This reflective study highlights the whole picture – past, present, and future. Many things in my life are still uncertain."

> BOB'S COMMENTARY: Contrary to popular belief, stages of grief do not exist. Everyone grieves differently and the feelings are not easily defined. Jim is learning to be as comfortable as he can with the uncertainty life brings him. At this point, going to work and being a father to his two grown children seems like his purpose now. By asking himself questions about his

feelings, the Inquire Within Program can help Jim understand where he is in the grief process, how he feels about his loss, and how he's dealing with it.

What other questions do you think Jim could ask himself? How do these questions apply to your life?

~ ~ ~ ~

Ling L.

Ling L. is a forty-five-year-old Jewish woman who has suffered from chronic back pain for several years. She has three teenage children and has been married for twenty years. Her physical pain not only affects her emotional world, but also impacts her job, her relationship with her husband, and raising her kids. She is willing to try different treatments to ease her pain and wants to be present as much as possible.

> BOB'S COMMENTARY: Ling's story is a great example of how one simple question can lead to pages of inner material. Delving into your emotional pain issues often involves returning to the same question over and over again until you discover clarity. In the following pages Ling explores issues, then turns to others, and eventually returns to those she previously touched upon. Repeating yourself is perfectly normal as your answer to a particular question becomes more refined and expansive. Sometimes we contradict ourselves within the same paragraph. Again, this is a natural way of working through issues. Note how Ling returns to the same themes with slightly different viewpoints.

Ling's Emotional Pain Question:

How am I coping with my physical pain?

"On most days I can manage the pain, but each day I have to deal with fatigue, discomfort, guilt, and the mental battle over whether or not I should take pain medication. The pain medication is addictive and I have to be careful how much I use. My father is an alcoholic and I'm afraid I could become addicted to these pills. But, I also have to weigh the need to be there for my family. Some days the pain is so bad, all I can do is lie down. On these days I have difficulty functioning without the medicine, so I'm conflicted about when I should use it.

"The process of finding what was actually wrong with me began when I blew out a disc in my back in 2006. I iced and used heat, but it didn't get any better. I used anti-inflammatories and epidurals (pain reducing injections). None of these treatments worked well.

"I felt hopeless and chose to have spinal fusion surgery. My disc is healed, but the surgery triggered a genetic disease called psoriatic arthritis. Psoriasis is a skin disease that causes red patches on the body, and this can sometimes cause arthritis. As with many other illnesses, the medical establishment isn't clear about how or why this happens.

"I told myself I would never have fusion surgery because it is major surgery and I worried about putting my family through this. I would be bedbound during recovery and need their help, unable to play the role of mother and wife. But finally I had no options. I could live with the debilitating pain that affected my mobility, mood, and outlook on life, or undergo the surgery.

"I felt the pain in my back, hips, hands, spine, neck, and I hurt everywhere. But with more aggressive treatment – pain medication, the pain has greatly decreased and I feel I can manage it well. I have a lot less swelling in my joints. However, I feel guilty about taking the medicine because I don't know the long-term effects.

This is a big issue for me. Ten years ago we didn't know over-the-counter medicines such as aspirin, Tylenol and Ibuprofen can destroy your internal organs. Aspirin can cause stomach bleeding and ulcers. Tylenol can cause liver damage, and Ibuprofen may impair your kidneys. Will I get cancer from the biologics?"

Other questions Ling might ask herself:

What effects did this struggle have on me emotionally?

Am I more fearful than before I began having back pain?

What strengths have I acquired since going through this journey?

> BOB'S COMMENTARY: Each of these questions will help Ling get in touch with the price she has paid and the life lessons she has learned from this debilitating physical pain.

"I wish I had an alternative to these meds, but I have to deal with what is. I have to accept that at times I need to take strong medications.

"Exercise does indeed help the pain. After being treated in January, I was reluctant to start exercising again because when the pain starts in one area it usually spreads to another. I was fearful exercise would make the pain worse and then I would become very emotional; a state I don't like being in. I then become moody, irritable, and difficult to be with. Then I have to take more pain medication and this becomes a frightening and depressing cycle.

"Yesterday I went back to my exercise routine, which involves swimming and the elliptical trainer. Today I feel much better, both mentally and physically. Something about swimming allows me to let go of things I want to get rid of. For me, exhaling into the water while I swim is pushing out all the bad stuff. This has always been therapeutic for me. I like the auditory experience where I hear my lungs blowing out the stress as I exhale into the water. I recently added my MP3 player to the mix and music is a great way of pushing you further when you're exhausted. Country music deals with loss and I strongly relate to it."

Other questions Ling could ask herself:

How could I use the calming experience in my everyday life that I get from swimming and listening to music?

How does country music help me grieve for my loss?"

> BOB'S COMMENTARY: These questions can help Ling discover tools to use when she's feeling fearful or hopeless about her physical condition. Feeling in touch with her emotional pain and what she has lost is an important step toward forming a realistic perspective of the physical pain.

"Sometimes when I became overwhelmed by pain and a sense of hopelessness, I would go to my room and cry. Then I'd call my husband, who uses humor as a way to distract me. When I'm crying so hard I can barely speak and I don't respond to him, he says, 'Honey, not the water works again!' His humor gets me out of the doldrums.

"Sometimes I don't want to talk about how anxious, depressed, or scared I feel because I don't want to burden anyone. I have the sense my family is sick of my complaining and don't want to hear it anymore. I also think they're worried about me and want to avoid those fearful feelings by not talking about them."

Other questions Ling could ask herself:

How do I know how my family feels about my illness?
How do they communicate how they feel about my condition?
Would it help to ask them how they feel about what's happening to me?

BOB'S COMMENTARY: These questions may lead to a family discussion about Ling's physical and emotional pain – Issues that family members have been keeping to themselves, such as their fear about Ling's health, may be raised. She could honestly respond to them by sharing her fears, hopes, and dreams about what's going on. This may bring the family closer and decrease the tension they experience on a daily basis.

"I am definitely doing better, but I have underlying guilt and worry about the possibility of the medication killing me during this process. I am on chemo medication called methotrexate, which is used to ease the symptoms of arthritis and MS. My disease is caused by an overactive immune system that is attacking my body, and methotrexate helps suppresses this reaction. One of the side effects from this drug is death. Doctors prescribe this medicine when they think nothing else will work.

"I now educate myself on different treatments. I continue expanding my knowledge of anatomy and biology to learn how the body works. In the beginning of my struggle, I didn't want to know what was going on and what kinds of treatments were being offered. I just wanted relief from my pain. They could have injected me with gasoline and I wouldn't have known the difference. Now, when I go to the doctor's office, I ask questions until I get an understanding of what they plan to do. Now I know it's important to be knowledgeable in order to make sound decisions regarding my health. So for six months, that is what I've done. I exercise a bit and I'm now working on the nutritional aspects of my illness.

"Sometimes I feel like a guinea pig trying all these different drugs. Every day I see Humira ads on television for a drug I take. The part of the ad that lists side effects takes most of the air time. I become anxious when I hear, "In rare cases, lymphoma can occur." Seeing this on television makes me angry.

"I always consider the quality of my life. Sometimes I want to do nothing but lie around in bed, but then my guilt kicks in. I feel I am not being productive or helpful to my family. Now my battle is to make myself exercise. I know it will help me, but I have trouble making myself follow through. I need to reach down deep to find the motivation."

Other questions Ling could ask herself:

Why do I feel so guilty much of the time?

Am I really guilty of something egregious?

Do I feel guilty because my physical symptoms don't always allow me to be consistent as a mom and a wife?

How can I alleviate my guilt?

> BOB'S COMMENTARY: Questions about dealing with guilt are always essential. Intense guilt can feel like your soul is being crushed. By asking questions about your guilt, you begin to determine what you're truly responsible for, versus issues you feel guilty about for which you should not be held accountable.

"Sometimes I'm exhausted from dealing with pain and side effects of the drugs. I try to avoid narcotics, but there are days that require me being energized for ten to twelve hours and the only way to function at that level is to take a narcotic. I don't want to tell my family I need down time, because I feel guilty.

"I feel guilty that I'm not as productive as a wife and parent should be. Most of the time, I function pretty well. I've done lots of counseling in my life and know that positive self-talk gets me through. But, there is the evil guy, the demon that haunts me."

Other questions Ling could ask herself:

What does the evil demon look like?

What is his true purpose?

What does he say to me and how can I neutralize him?

> BOB'S COMMENTARY: These questions help us face the demons we all have inside. By asking these questions, we can understand what the demons are trying to accomplish. Some call the demons our dark side, whose words are designed to create self-hate and doubt. If we face these demons instead of ignoring them, we can learn to make peace with this troubling part of ourselves.

"I feel angry because I'm forty-five years old and sometimes I feel like I'm eighty. I'm trying to accept what is. Sometimes I think I do accept my predicament, but other times I feel lost and I falter. I want to find peace.

"Where is the place inside where I can come to terms and find peace with this? What does that place look like? How will I deal with it once I get there? These are questions I should take a look at.

"I feel worried and anxious much of the time. I woke up Friday with a migraine headache and gave myself shots of the medicine for the pain. I ended up in the emergency room. They told me to get my sinuses checked to make sure I didn't have an infection. They ended up injecting me with steroids-prednisone, and then I begin feeling the bloat. My eating habits were getting more compulsive and I couldn't figure out why. It dawned on me that the steroids were making me eat compulsively.

"I exercised the next day and felt much better. So, instead of panicking and freaking out, I calmly analyzed my situation and took appropriate action."

Other questions Ling could ask herself:

How do I deal with the uncertainty my precarious health situation brings?

How do I learn to deal with new aches and pains?

> BOB'S COMMENTARY: These questions are important for anyone who suffers from chronic pain. Ling is learning how to deal with new aches and pains without panicking. She is also learning not to emotionally fixate on her back pain, because that only makes the throbbing feel worse. She also knows it's important to cultivate a positive attitude. No matter how down she feels, she can reach for that place where she feels she will someday find the assistance she needs. While she may never be totally pain free and may always be dependent on heavy duty medication, she can still have a great quality of life with the hope she will continue to improve.

"My family is supportive of me when I hit rock bottom. This is when I get emotional, cry easily, grab my ice packs, and take to the bed. When I have a major flare-up my kids do their best to help me. They bring me ice packs and other things I need. They leave me alone to recuperate.

"I do have faith at times and ask for help. This seems to help and the pain decreases."

> BOB'S COMMENTARY: Ling's depiction of dealing with chronic pain is in solidarity with other folks who experience the same issues. However, asking the question of how she was handling it helped her determine she was coping very well. She also realized that coping with it didn't mean eliminating the chronic pain; it meant managing the pain well.

"My oldest daughter is one of the laziest people on the planet, yet demanding work from her when I can't do any work myself seems like a double standard. She's close to being pushed out of our home because she takes too much for granted and isn't pulling her weight.

"I decided to leave my parent's home as soon as I was able because of the chaos around their divorce. My daughter may be following in my footsteps, albeit this is a different situation. She is lucky because she doesn't have to face adversity the way I did.

"I find it hard to be consistent with parenting, especially making sure the kids are doing their chores and homework. Sometimes I'm right on top of it, while at other times I'm lost in my pain and not checking in with them. I know they are aware of my inconsistencies, but I wonder what they actually think about all this. I am wondering if they think I'm a lazy parent.

"My husband has learned to adapt to my situation. We have always had lots of independence in our marriage. He is very active and I could never meet his energy level even before my back injury. I sometimes have to force myself to participate in activities with him. At times I enjoy this, and sometimes I don't. I plan my time around my husband's schedule.

"I realize I am okay and actually doing pretty well. I think a support group would be helpful for dealing with the guilt. The guilt is based on fear and not being able to do things I want to do. At times I feel too filled with pain and fear to go about my planned day, but I feel I don't have a choice. At this point the merging of physical pain, fear, hopelessness, and guilt kick in all at once. I need to find a new way to handle all this.

"Usually I can tell myself everything is okay. This is not my fault, and I don't have any control over what's going on with me physically. But, sometimes it's all too much. However, I am thankful for what I do have and I can build on that."

BOB'S COMMENTARY: Ling's story is a great example of how one question can lead to so much inner material to look at. Delving into your emotional pain issues often involves returning to the same question over and over again until you discover clarity. Ling explores issues then turns to others and eventually returns to those she previously touched upon. It is perfectly natural and normal to repeat questions, because your answer will then become more refined and expansive.

What other questions could Ling could ask herself? How do these apply to your life?

~ ~ ~ ~

Lisa M.

Lisa M. is a forty-seven-year-old African-American woman who lives in New Orleans and is almost ready to graduate from junior college. As she struggles with codependence issues, the Inquire Within Program is helping her work through her memories and feelings. She is recently divorced and has no children.

"My safe space is the center of my heart. This is where God resides for me. It is also the place where my true being lives. I was raised as a Baptist and have tried to follow my upbringing. However, I found the hypocrisy of the church conflicts with what I feel serving God means."

Emotional Pain Question:

Why do I try so hard to please others when I only hurt myself in the end?

"I think it has to do with the way I was raised. I was the oldest child of four in a Southern Baptist Christian family. My mother and grandmother always taught me to do the right thing. Now that I'm older I want to do the right thing, but the definition of the right thing has changed. When I was growing up, it meant doing all you could for someone else and ignoring your own needs. Now I want to get my own needs met and not worry about taking care of others.

"Sacrificing myself comes from being an African-American female entrenched in the Southern Baptist Christian religion. Living this way led me to feel miserable, and that's still true in my present situation. I decided to live with my 89-year-old infirm aunt in order to be her caretaker. There was a voice telling me this was a bad idea, but I decided to live with her anyhow because she was there for me when I needed her. However, she is cantankerous, judgmental, and insensitive to my feelings."

Other questions Lisa could ask herself:

How did the hypocrisy I observed in the church affect me as a child?

How did the teachings of the church play a role in my becoming a codependent?

> BOB'S COMMENTARY: These questions will help anyone who has been adversely affected by organized religion. Lisa realizes that life in the Southern Baptist Church deeply influenced her opinions and attitudes as she was growing up. Now, she realizes much of what she learned was dysfunctional and she is reinventing herself.

"I thought living with her was going to be one way, and it actually turned out to be another. My aunt accused me of hating her brother, which was a huge insult to me. To accuse me of hating another person feels like she's attacking my character. I may dislike someone intensely, but I don't hate anyone. That is too strong a word to describe my feelings."

Other questions Lisa could ask herself:

Am I too sensitive?

Do I allow myself to be hurt too deeply by what others think of me?

> BOB'S COMMENTARY: These are questions anyone who is codependent can ask. These questions can lead to others, such as "How do I know if I'm too sensitive or not?" "Am I preoccupied by worrying about pleasing other folks even if I really don't like all of them?" These questions will help you recognize what emotional support you need from others, and know that we can all reach inside to boost our self-esteem.

"When I put someone's needs ahead of my own, I end up feeling either unhappy or resentful. In these situations, when I give of myself my giving isn't reciprocated. For example, when I moved in with my aunt, several of her relatives committed themselves to helping her. One of her daughters planned to go food shopping and another son promised to take her to doctors appointments. However, neither of these folks has come through, so it's all left on me to take care of.

"When I call them, they say they forgot and I should call sooner to remind them. I don't have time to remind them! I'm a full time student and this takes most of my time. I am aiming to obtain a 3.5 GPA because I know that's what will take me to the next level – and an excellent four year college."

> BOB'S COMMENTARY: Codependence is a state of being experienced by many women in different cultures. Women are taught they should sacrifice themselves for the greater good: husband, family, and anyone else in need. Women learn to deny their own needs. In fact,

they learn not to have any needs at all and simply live to fulfill other's needs. Here, Lisa learns from her work in the past that she has the right to recognize her needs and the freedom to get those needs met.

"My relatives say to me, 'You're doing a real good job in taking care of your aunt.' These words are meaningless to me. I don't need kudos. I need help.

"I tend to attract people who want someone to take care of them without giving anything back. I think I do this because of what happened when I was a young child. I'm two years older than my sister, and when my mother brought her home for the first time, she said to me, 'She's your baby.' That gave me the message that I was a second mother to my sister. I felt I was responsible for her. When she got in trouble, I would interrogate her about her choices. This continued for years."

Other questions Lisa could ask herself:

How can I tell which people in my life will be strictly takers and which ones will be open to a more equal relationship?

Do I have to rush into any relationship?

What is it like to take things slow?

> BOB'S COMMENTARY: These are great questions for anyone who wants to approach relationships in a healthy way.

"Ten years later, my mother had a second set of kids. Then I had two smaller sisters to look after and I also felt a deep sense of responsibility toward them.

"I always seemed to put them first and ignore my own needs, which set me on the path to being codependent. I would take on others' stuff and focus on them rather than myself. I took on all the negative energy from my family and other relationships. I had no idea what I was doing or why.

"In a family, everyone has a position and those who never experienced that particular position don't know what it's like. As the oldest sibling, a huge burden was placed on my shoulders and I don't feel my family was aware of that or cared how it affected me.

"So I ask myself, 'Why do I keep setting myself up for the same thing when I already know the outcome?' I continually repeat this pattern because I know it's the right thing to do for others. I feel obligated to do for others and the pressure to do so comes from me internally as well as from external forces.

"Even in a relationship with a man, I've noticed I repeat the same pattern. I went looking for one thing – love and validation, and ended up with another – spending all my time trying to meet his unrealistic needs. I wanted the strong male, an alpha male who would take care of things, but now I realize they have their own issues trying to be the alpha. For years with my former husband, I tried to show him what a good woman I was. 'See, I can cook, clean, and take care of your adult kids.' But nothing I did was good enough and he was harshly critical of me.

"So I learned the whole concept of the alpha male is false. It's like putting a crown on the poorest man in the world and calling him a king. I've always been attracted to people who need something."

Other questions Lisa could ask herself:

Why am I attracted to partners who need something and are incapable of giving me anything?

> BOB'S COMMENTARY: This question will help Lisa understand she's attracted to emotionally unavailable people because she's used to dealing with men who have this quality. She hates this

drill, but knows how it works. She also learns that sometimes we seek primary relationships with people who share the dysfunctional qualities our parents had. This happens because we're accustomed to dealing with our parents and the emotional terrian seems familiar. We may also act out an unconcious desire to change our partner's selfish personality. Some of us feel if we can change that person, he will be grateful and suddenly approve of our existance. Some of us feel if we change our partner, we can change our parents as well, and then they will finally love us. Of course this never happens except in fairy tales. So, the work is to realize we deserve to be loved, no matter how awful our childhood.

"It's important that someone in my family get a college degree and I am driven to do so. I am learning to say no to others' requests. The fact that people in my circle aren't used to me denying their requests makes it much harder to do so. However, it's getting easier.

"My aunt has been the matriarch of our family for many years and always had the last word on decisions. Now I am continually challenging those choices if I don't think they make sense or if they have a negative impact on me.

"I used to think that doing for others was love. Now I realize it wasn't love. They don't love me any more if I do the stuff or if I don't. There were times when I gave into the demands or requests of others to do things for them, because saying no would tear me up inside and I worried about whether they still liked me or were mad at me. Now, when I say no it doesn't have the same effect. I don't feel all torn up inside and I just go about my business.

"I now have my eyes set on Tulane University. I know you're supposed to apply to many colleges, but I have my heart set on

Tulane because I feel like it's home. When I toured the campus and classrooms, I felt a comfort level knowing this is the right place.

"Sometimes I have anxiety spells where I get the heart palpitations and all that. But, my mind also races and I get exhausted and need to lie down. Emotional Freedom Technique (EFT), Yoga, and meditation have helped me. I've had to learn how to be with myself. My current goal is to go to the movies by myself. I can go to a restaurant alone now and that was a huge fear previously. I want to learn to live totally independent.

"Learning to be independent and do things on my own is difficult, because I was taught to take care of others. I wasn't taught how to take care of myself. I know if I go out for a walk I will feel better, but I'm not doing it. I sometimes feel sorry for myself and lie on the bed and cry. I'll talk on the phone and complain about my situation, or watch TV. I know none of this helps me, so I need to do something else – something that will help me.

"Living with my aunt triggers all this stuff from my childhood. I constantly feel shamed and ridiculed. My aunt worries about something different every day. I have to work hard not to take that worry on. Life is too short for all that worry and I have too much to do.

"I took a holistic health class and a stress management class. I'm doing things to improve my mental health. There has to be a better way of living than the way I was taught, because the way I was taught to live sucks.

"In the past I had a fantasy that if I really came through and delivered what folks desired, then they would truly love me and I would no longer have to long for their affection. But now I realize they aren't going to love me any more or less no matter what I do. This has been a very freeing insight.

"My aunt has a reputation at church for being a kind person. I have found this is not accurate and she spends a lot of time telling me I'm going to hell. This has caused me to rethink my whole belief system regarding organized religion. It doesn't work for me. I feel the God of my heart wants me to do something good every day. So if I'm doing something good for mankind every day, why do I have to sit in a building with a bunch of hypocrites who would talk bad about me if they didn't like my clothes, my makeup, or my voice is too loud? I choose not to be part of this any longer.

"I keep setting myself up because I'm still searching for a response from people that wasn't fulfilled earlier in my life. I'm beginning to understand that I had certain beliefs that were not true. I spent time with my sister yesterday and she told me she didn't like to be touched on her elbows – that it made her uncomfortable. Matter of fact, she told me she didn't like folks to be too affectionate with her. She felt uncomfortable when she was hugged too long.

"I said, 'I don't know how that happened because Momma was affectionate.' My mother chimed in to say she wasn't affectionate at all. I've been beating myself up over my lack of affection with my nieces and nephews. I thought something was wrong with me and that I had been taught differently. Now, with this new information, I could begin to understand why I wasn't affectionate. It's because my mother wasn't physically warm with me.

"I'm finally asking questions about issues that have haunted me since I was a child. One question I asked was: 'What did I do to seduce my older neighbor to molest me?' He was a child three years older than me. I always believed I had enticed him. I have finally come to understand I am not to blame for his molesting me; he is to blame. I let go of this and released it.

"Organized religion also contributed to my skewed way of thinking about this. The church people were always talking about fast tailed little girls. They had rigidly defined roles for men, women, boys, and girls. I used to feel I was one of those fast girls until I started therapy.

"Another question I asked myself is: 'What happened to my marriage?' I learned my ex-husband was not an honest person and was incapable of empathizing with me. He was fine being with me until the money got tight and credit went bad. After that he left. When I realized I was used, I felt deeply hurt. Now I feel I'm recovering from that. Though I'm ready for a new relationship, right now I'm okay with being on my own.

"My mother spent a lot of time with her girls and she would take us to plays and museums. My father was in plays. My mother taught us to think of others and she taught us to have a voice. She didn't have much of a voice herself. My mother was reluctant to speak up because she hated confrontation. My sisters and I hate confrontation as well, but we will speak up when necessary. She gave us a good foundation, but she didn't provide us with the tools of how to confront others. It is a good thing to speak up for yourself, but not to argue for argument's sake.

"The stereotype for Black people is that we are loud, unemployed, uneducated, and ignorant. So asserting myself may convince people that I am that stereotype, and I don't want others to think that way of me.

"I find it easy to fall back into the old codependent way, which is what I did by moving in with my aunt. I wanted my aunt to be comfortable and not have to move out of her house into a board and care home, or worse, a nursing home. This was a difficult decision because it largely went against my better judgment, but I didn't want her to have to leave her home. I gave my happiness for hers and I've been miserable ever since.

"My aunt, although highly critical of me, was there for me when I was young. She gave me money and a place to stay when I needed help. I also paid her back the money I borrowed. I knew from the get-go that living with her wasn't the right decision for me, but it was the right thing to do for her.

"I'm plagued with insomnia, anxiety, and depression and I take medication for all of them. I am searching for alternatives to the medicine. I've recently found that deep breathing helps tremendously and lets me fall asleep. The medications are helpful, but now that I'm doing so much better I want to wean myself off them. I want to get to the place where I can mediate and find that spot where I feel secure.

"My confidence level has improved tremendously with my experiences at junior college. I was always a C student and thought I had average intelligence. Now I think I'm very smart and I got a 3.0 GPA last semester. That boost of confidence gives me faith I will do well in the future.

"I don't have the need for others to validate my accomplishments. I'm proud of myself and I can celebrate this all by myself without looking for kudos from others."

> BOB'S COMMENTARY: Lisa learned from completing this exercise that her codependence was created by several factors involving her sex, race, and religion. Understanding this process helped her unravel her feelings, so she can now distinguish between what others want and what she desires.

What other questions could Lisa ask herself? How do these apply to your life?

~ ~ ~ ~

Bob Livingstone

Emotional Pain Question:

Why do I keep feeling I'm emotionally stuck?

"I marvel at the fact that I run 25 miles per week, enjoy my work as a therapist and writer and take no medicine (for now). I do take a bunch of supplements. I am blessed to have a great marriage and wonderful friends with whom I celebrate life.

"But, I realize I've been burdened with being in a state of emotional limbo since I was an adolescent. When I was around 15 (it was so long ago, I'm not sure exactly how old I was) my father was angry at me for some reason and blundered into my room with the intention of beating me. He took a menacing stance, but instead of him putting his hands on me, I punched him in the stomach. I braced myself for his inevitable retaliation, but his reaction was much worse than that: he just stared through me like I was invisible, then turned and walked away. He never really talked to me again. He just looked at me like I shouldn't and didn't exist.

"I realize now this was the pivotal moment where I crossed the line with him. The divide between disappointment and disdain had been obliterated.

"I've spent the rest of my life attempting to deal with the guilt, fear, and self-hatred this event evoked. I have tried to complete this by talking to his spirit and by taking on too much work in an effort to be seen as a good person, not a reckless teenager who punches his sick father.

"I didn't know he was sick until after his death. He had several TIAs and eventually died from a stroke. I remember him holding his head because the headaches were so painful. He had no patience for me or my sister. I wasn't aware at the time that he was slowly losing his mind; something I deeply fear might happen to me.

"He forgot to tell his boss he was going on vacation; how does that happen? His brain must have been deteriorating. Why didn't anyone do anything about this? There was no support for my mother, sister, or me. I felt totally alone and I still feel that way much of the time. I'm still afraid at letting others get too close to me, because if I allow that to happen they may be taken away from me and I'll be all alone with no barrier from the world's ills.

"When I do take the risk of letting down my guard, I'm overwhelmed by the beauty of my connections with my wife, friends, family, and clients. This is similar to listening to a moving song that opens your heart and captures your freedom.

"So I am capable of being intimate. I just don't allow it to happen as frequently as I need and want. At age 60, it's time for that to change.

"My father died when he was 56 and I am now 60. On some level, I feel guilty that I have been on this planet longer than him. I also had a series of health problems that caused me to feel it was my destiny to die before age 56, or at least not too long after.

"Is what I am experiencing prolonged, stuck grief or am I simply ready to step into deeper terrain around the story of my father's death? I know our relationships with dead loved ones change as we grow into different developmental stages. We also perceive events of our lives differently as we age.

"My immediate answer to this question is that I'm stuck, but that is the voice of the guilt ridden, self-loathing child coming out. As I wrote in an earlier article, the concept of closure around loss is a myth.

"I'm trying to place my father and my memories of him in a safe, sacred space inside me. At different times I discover this space only for him to return to a place of haunting, burdening, unforgiving, and loss to me.

"I don't think we ever truly accept that one of our loved ones is dead. Can we accept that we are going to die some day? I believe the answer is no.

"I keep him alive by living the guilt, hopelessness, and perpetual angst. At times I cannot separate his incomplete life from my own very complete one.

"Every time I see one of those movies that take place in the 1950s where the men fail to reach their dreams, I shudder because that was my dad's life.

"But it is not my life and I have the right to my own dreams. I have the right to love and be loved. I can love my father for all that he was. I don't have to piecemeal it in order to dissect his being. I see him at peace and smiling with my mother up in the blue sky just above the Golden Gate Bridge.

"So forget closure, acceptance, or any other words that mean the end. It suddenly dawns on me that I will never find peace if I believe there is nothing after death; that there is no afterlife; that there is no God or Heaven.

"During my entire life I thought the concept of an afterlife made no sense. It was illogical. Perhaps the existence of God makes this incomplete life go full circle. Perhaps it makes more sense than I thought."

What other questions could Bob ask himself? How to they apply to your situation?

Chapter 6
Review of Case Studies

E xamining your own behavior, values, and the source of your emotional pain requires courage. You'll need both perseverance and patience to find solutions to these problems. Practicing the Inquire Within Program will take you to the point of resolving internal conflicts and finding happiness. This doesn't mean we discover perfection and never experience fear or confusion again. It does mean we can learn to minimize the time, frequency, and intensity of this negative space.

In Chapter Five we met people who were willing to pursue this challenging process. They were able to face, explore, and understand their emotional pain by asking questions about it. They made personal discoveries in all aspects of the program, which includes...

- Finding your Internal Safe Space,
- Creating your Calming Music Play List,

- The Inquire Within Questionnaire,
- The Internal Therapist, and
- The What if It Were Someone Else and Not You Exercise.

The art of asking the right emotional pain question is the heart of this book. Honestly asking yourself if you're unhappy and delving into the reasons why can open new vistas of understanding and hope in your life. Several of the men and women in these case studies were able to reflect on their previous unhappiness and trace the steps they made to increase their sense of contentment. Most were able to pinpoint the source of their unhappiness after they asked the question, "Am I unhappy?" Somehow, the simple act of asking this question opened a door to the answers. Once they are able to determine the source of unhappiness, they make action plans to change these feelings.

Just as each of the case study participants benefited from Inquire Within, you can use the information in this chapter as a guide for your personal work. Hopefully, the examples and comments will help you learn to ask the right self-questions.

~ ~ ~ ~

Mary B. and Relationships

Mary B. is a 28-year-old Latina woman who has difficulty with primary relationships because of her parents' hostile separation and divorce. Through Inquire Within she found serenity in the internal safe space and listening to her calming music play list. She learned that most of us don't take enough time to be quiet and listen to ourselves. Doing so helped her feel grounded and able to face her emotional pain.

Self-questioning also showed Mary a connection between trying to placate her two unhappy parents and going over the top to please her partners in present time. She looked at how she unknowingly sabotaged relationships in the past out of fear they might not work, or fear she would let down her guard, allow herself to be intimate, and in the end would be abandoned.

Questioning herself also made Mary aware that she does want to have a great relationship with a partner someday and is willing to look at the fear surrounding this possibility.

Like Mary, if we can look at our fears by asking questions about them, we stand a good chance of finding answers. Mary learned that her parents' crumbling marriage and hostile relationship taught her to be reactive rather than strategic. She is finding ways to slow things down and think about a response to a situation rather than just going with her first impulse.

~ ~ ~ ~

Melinda's Emotional Pain

Melinda M. is a 32 year old Puerto-Rican woman who grew up with an alcoholic mother who yelled and hit Melinda when she felt chores were not done correctly. Melinda felt her mother didn't nurture her.

In this program, one special question can lead to a lengthy answer that contains many thoughts, observations, and insights. These insights can bring huge progress in one afternoon. Melinda's first emotional pain question was: "What obstacles in my childhood do I need to overcome in order to move forward as an adult?"

This question led to many revelations for Melinda. She learned she was in a state of constant inner conflict – a state many of us experience. It's important to normalize this experience, not demonize it. She realized her poverty, not having a father around, and her mother's rage made her feel she didn't fit in anywhere.

Melinda didn't feel accepted as a child, as a teenager, and during most of her adult life. She wants to confront her mother about her feelings, but is afraid it will be an exercise in futility. She's afraid her mother will not honor her feelings about the abuse.

She learned it was safe to be invisible so she wouldn't be emotionally hurt, but being invisible meant no one noticed all the good things she did. She has learned she needs to change her focus from looking to others for approval to looking inward for answers. She learned from this Inquire Within exercise that she no longer wants to walk on egg shells, and she now has faith that she can accomplish this.

~ ~ ~ ~

Jim G's Terrible Loss

Jim G's wife died after being run down by a car. He knows this is the source of his unhappiness, but he doesn't know if he'll ever again find the joy he had with her. He finds solace in studying the nature of life and the humans who have to deal with it. For example, he says, "If I love, I will ultimately grieve." He realizes he feels shattered and is learning to find his pace in seeking alternatives to mourning. The act of asking and answering emotional pain questions is a means for healing his grief. He combines this with mindfulness techniques that teach us thoughts are random and you don't need to lock them in your psyche.

Jim has become aware that not knowing who his father was caused him to be self-critical and he often beats himself up. He also feels his mother was never emotionally available. Jim learned not to give these negative thoughts power, because if he does he will obsess about them. If he gives them no power, they flow through him and go away.

Although Jim doesn't appear to have much hope or direction for his future, he is now looking outside the realm of pure survival. He isn't sure what's possible, but not ready to give up. The Inquire Within Program provided him with an assessment of where he is emotionally. He found this was a painful experience with a lot of uncertainty. Hopefully he will find contentment in the future.

~ ~ ~ ~

Aida C. - a Survivor

Aida C, a survivor of horrible abuse, stated that listening to her calming music play list releases some of the pain she remembers from childhood. She wasn't aware of her readiness to deeply examine her unhappiness, but once she asked herself the happiness question her emotional pain exploded front and center.

When Aida asked herself why she was unhappy, she admitted for the first time that she experienced ongoing physical, sexual, and emotional abuse as a child. She then decided to look deeper inside and understand how this degradation affected her. Hopefully, accepting the fact that the abuse occurred will help her feel ready to share it with her therapist and close friends.

Aida was brave enough to dig deep inside and try to understand the reasons for her inability to trust anyone. She learned that being abandoned, neglected, and abused by her parents and other adults caused her to rely only on herself.

As a child she believed she wasn't old or wise enough to be a good teacher to herself. She expressed anger and dismay at being treated in such a disparaging way. Inquire Within was a cathartic experience for her. She was honest about how angry she felt and that she had been a violent gang member in the past. She has also been incarcerated, but now – through her own inner strength – she is close to finishing law school.

She realizes she learned how to parent from her parents and they were the worst possible role models. She knows she wants to change this pattern, and has done so.

Aida reached to the bottom of her soul here: she delivered brutal honesty derived from one self-question: "Why are you unhappy?" She discussed how hard it was never to be an innocent child and how gaining weight gives her a sense of safety. It also causes isolation and depression, but her whole emphasis was on survival. She still feels that way for the most part, but she now has a man in her life and feels this is the first healthy relationship she has ever experienced. All her primary relationships in the past have led to becoming a domestic violence victim. This new relationship is devoid of physical violence. She's afraid to tell him about her sordid past, but she's building up to it.

~ ~ ~ ~

Ling L. and Chronic Pain

Ling L. is a forty-five-year-old Jewish woman who has struggled for several years with chronic back pain and its affect on her life. At times the debilitating pain prevents her from doing anything more than lying in bed. She felt she had to enlist all her strength to ask the emotional pain question, "How am I coping with my physical pain?"

This may be a common question for chronic pain sufferers, but do they ask with the purpose of discovering an answer, or is it a question filled with panic that only leads to more anxiety?

Ling seriously assessed how she's coping and how she processes daily management of her pain. She struggles with how much pain medication to take each day. Sometimes taking the medication is the only way to meet family obligations. Then there's the issue of doing too much while medicated and feeling terrible the next day. She was able to connect her father's alcoholism with the possibility that she could become addicted to pain meds. Her sense of dignity comes through clearly and affirmatively here. The Inquire Within program helped her look at pain realistically, with a hopeful direction.

She talked about her different treatments and diagnoses and, like other case study participants, she was able to track her progress and honor her struggle.

Ling shared the difficulty her injury and pain management create for her husband and children. She feels they all shared a diagnosis of post traumatic stress disorder (PTSD), an anxiety disorder that may occur after witnessing or experiencing a traumatic event. She realized she needs to deal with her guilt about taking medication and at times feeling she isn't there for her family. She is considering a support group and/or individual counseling.

By helping her ask the question "How am I coping with my pain?" the Inquire Within Program helped Ling realize that pain management is a balancing act that includes exercise, pain meds, support, self-advocacy, maintaining a positive attitude, educating yourself about your condition, and not being afraid to ask questions.

~ ~ ~ ~

Lisa M. and Codependence

Lisa M. is a forty-seven-year-old African-American woman who struggles with codependence issues. Codependence is an extreme act of taking care of other's needs while totally ignoring your own.

Lisa's emotional pain question was, "Why do I try so hard to please others when I only hurt myself in the end?" This question allowed Lisa to look into her childhood for answers. She felt that religion, the role of black women, and her mother giving her the message that her younger sisters were her responsibility, all contributed to her codependence. She realizes she is tired of taking care of others and now wants to take care of herself, something she's just beginning to learn how to do.

The Inquire Within program taught Lisa that present circumstances can trigger unresolved issues from the past. Lisa recently moved in with her rigid, controlling aunt and this reminded her of her oppressive childhood where she was expected to take care of others, but receive no acknowledgement for her efforts. She also learned the price she paid, and is still paying, for putting others first and ignoring her own needs. She often feels unhappy and regretful.

She discovered that going to junior college and obtaining high grades is a clear indicator she is taking care of herself for the first time in her life. She fights against all those in her family who try to derail her goal of a college degree.

The Inquire Within Program helped Lisa determine she previously tended to seek love from those she took care of. She now realizes that being used in this manner has nothing to do with love. She is on a path to finding out what love truly is.

Chapter 7

Let's Begin to Inquire Within

Instructions for completing the Inquire Within Program

*P*lease read the entire book before you start the program. After you finish reading the book, return to this chapter and begin the Inquire Within exercises.

The program consists of the following exercises:
- The Inquire Within Questionnaire will teach you how to ask emotional pain questions,
- The Internal Psychotherapist teaches you how to ask questions like a therapist,
- The If It Were Someone Else and Not You Exercise helps you learn to look at yourself from an outside perspective.

In the beginning of the program you'll be asked to find your internal safe space and create a musical play list. Then you'll be asked to complete all the exercises. This works best if you take your time and treat the exercises as a gift to yourself instead of a mandatory assignment. You will feel less pressure if you view this experience as one of personal growth instead of unbridled desperation.

After completing all the exercises, you may determine one of the three works better for you than the others. You may also feel parts of the exercises stimulate you, while other sections don't work as well. Feel free to repeat the sections of Inquire Within you find most effective. Chapter 7: The Inquire Within Program, Part Two shows the process for continuing this program after you complete the initial questions and answers.

I suggest you use the program at least once a week for a month, or until you have a chance to complete all the exercises. Then read over your notes and assess your progress by noticing what issues have transformed from confusion to clarity. Have you reached your goal of formulating and answering questions that alleviate your emotional pain? From your written work, can you see how you accomplished this? Do you feel more confidence and self-esteem?

This journey may be filled with angst and perplexity, but sticking with it gives you the opportunity to discover real joy within yourself.

The Inquire Within Program

If you'd like to print the Inquire Within questionnaire
worksheets, find the link at
http://www.unchainthepain.info/worksheets.html

Finding your Internal Safe Space and Creating your Calming Music Play List

An internal safe space is a location you can access inside your mind, body, and spirit that fills you with calmness and serenity. You will use this safe space as a retreat when overwhelming and frightening feelings emerge during the Inquire Within Program. During visits to your safe place, try to be in touch with all your senses, including your breathing, hearing, sight, and smells.

Imagine your safe space and describe it:

What do you see?

What do you hear?

What do you smell?

Why are you safe here?

List five to ten songs that will help you feel calm and reassured. Create your play list and listen to it.

1.

2.

3.

4.

5.

6.

7.

8.

9.

10.

Write about your experience while in your safe space:

How do you feel when you're here?

Talk about your experiences while listening to your calming music playlist:

How does the music make you feel?

Do you find these exercises helpful? If so, how?

The Inquire Within Questionnaire

The main purpose of this questionnaire is to help you ask probing questions and find what is actually troubling you. Once you uncover these old feelings, problems, and memories, you can discover how to find joy in your life. Now it's time for you to dive into the questionnaire.

1. In your opinion, are you unhappy too much of the time? Do you want to be happier more often?

2. What thoughts and feelings come up for you around unhappiness?

3. Do any of these emotional states apply to you? (circle those that apply and try to use them in your questions and answers)
    - Depressed
    - Anxious
    - Hopeless

4. What is the first question you want to ask yourself about your unhappiness? (Don't be surprised if one question leads to another during this process. Feel free to go with the flow.) Don't hesitate to respond to these questions with lengthy replies, if you wish.

5. What are the follow-up questions and answers about being unhappy? Please be paitent with yourself, because the questions and answers may not come quickly. Try to be tolerant of the silence that comes before thoughts and

feelings are produced. Sit with yourself for a while and allow questions and answers to arise.)

6. Do you feel emotionally stuck?

7. What are your thoughts and feelings about being emotionally stuck?

8. Do any of these emotional states apply to you? Circle those that apply and try to use them in your questions and answers.
   - Feeling disconnected from others.
   - Bored much of the time.
   - Fixated on a person or event.

9. Allow yourself to focus on feeling stuck and observe what memories, feelings, and other thoughts come up.

10. What is the first question you want to ask yourself about being emotionally stuck?

11. What is the answer?

12. What are the follow-up questions and answers about being emotionally stuck?

13. Do you feel like you are not present much of the time?

14. What are thoughts and feelings about living in the present?

15. Do any of these emotional states apply to you? Circle those that apply to you and use them in your questions and answers.

- Dwelling on the past.
- Worrying about the future.
- Dreading the day.

16. What is it like when you're able to concentrate on what's immediately going on inside and outside you?

17. What is the first question you want to ask yourself about living in the present?

18. Do you have problems maintaining intimate relationships?

19. What are your thoughts and feelings about intimate relationships?

20. Do any of these emotional states apply to you? Circle those that apply and use them in your questions and answers.
    - Agitation.
    - Blaming others for my difficulties with relationships.
    - Feeling empty.

21. Focus on what it's like to have difficulty maintaining a loving relationship with a partner. What is the first question you want to ask yourself? What are the follow-up questions?

22. Do you have a passion for anything?

23. What are your thoughts and feelings about having passion?

24. Focus on the fact that you aren't excited about much of anything. Think about the narrow range of emotions you experience.

25. What is the first question you want to ask yourself about passion?

26. What is the answer?

27. What follow-up questions do you want to ask yourself, and what are the answers?

The Internal Psychotherapist

When you seek help, you're hoping to find a professional who can provide relief from suffering – someone who can understand, empathize, and offer you the benefits of experience. The Internal Therapist teaches you to perform many of these functions yourself. Your instructions are to answer these sample questions and then formulate your own questions and answers.

1. Imagine you're in a therapist's office and think about the questions she may ask you. What is the first question she might ask?

2. What is your answer?

The next step in the Internal Therapist process is to identify an unhappy emotional state, such as...
  • I feel exhausted much of the time.
  • I worry constantly about my future.
  • I have difficulty letting go of unhealthy relationships.

Write your unhappy emotional state here:

3. Ask yourself, "What happened to cause this emotional state?"

4. Ask yourself, "Why did this happen?"

The third step in the Internal Therapist section is to ask leading questions, such as...
  • Why do I feel this way?"
  • How did this happen?"
  • How have I dealt with it in the past?"
  • How will I deal with it in the future?"
  • What do I believe in?"

5. What are some other leading questions? Write them down, along with the answers.

6. Then focus on your thinking process (your mind), your feeling and emotional processes (your body and mind), and your spiritual process (your soul). Write about each of these.

7. The next step is discovering your compassion, humanity, problem-solving ability, and ability to ask the right questions about your emotional pain.

8. Ask yourself and answer "Why do I have difficulty being compasionate toward myself?"

9. Ask yourself and answer "Am I a good problem solver?" "If not, why is that so and what can I do to improve in this area?"

10. Ask yourself and answer "Am I able to ask the right questions about my emotional pain?" "If so, how have I demonstrated that?" "If not, how can I improve?"

11. Empathize with your own struggles by asking yourself and answering, "Do I now realize how difficult it has been for me?"

12. Address painful childhood memories. "What is my most painful childhood memory?"

The "If It Were Someone Else and Not You" Exercise

This exercise is designed to help you see your emotional strengths, fears, and pain from an objective viewpoint.

Relax, take a few deep breaths, and use a relaxation exercise of your choice. Place yourself in a frame of mind whereby *you see yourself through the eyes of an objective, kind, and loving, presence outside yourself.* Focus on your qualities, but distance yourself from the questions *by pretending you're talking about someone else you know well.*

Spend as much time as you need on each question and note the following:

- How often do you talk about this person in a harsh way?
- If you do spend a lot of time talking about this person in a harsh way, explain why.
- How often do you talk about this person in a positive way? Why do you do this?

Now ask yourself these questions:

1. How old is this person?
2. What does he look like?
3. What does he do well?
4. What are his dreams?
5. What has prevented him from living his dreams?
6. Does he blame this on himself or others?
7. What are his close relationships like?
8. What is he afraid of and how does this affect him?
9. How does he deal with anger and sadness?
10. What events have had the greatest impact on his life?
11. Are you learning anything new about yourself from this exercise?

NOTES

Chapter 8

The Inquire Within Program,
Part Two

After completing the Inquire Within Program, you'll want to fine-tune the techniques for future use. Perhaps you found special parts of the program were more effective for you than others. Certain sections of particular exercises may resonate with you and stimulate new insight and discoveries. For example, perhaps you found the first part of The Internal Therapist extremely helpful, but the rest of that exercise didn't move you.

If so, you should focus on the first part of the exercise, which is...

- Imagine you're in a therapist's office and think about the questions she might ask you.
- What is the first question she may ask?
- What is your answer?

If you want to use this part of the exercise repeatedly and you're satisfied with your progress, then continue the process. When it's no longer beneficial, check out other parts of Inquire Within and give them a try.

Using the entire Inquire Within Program, I learned that health problems over the past couple of years caused me to feel anxious and depressed. When I asked myself if I was unhappy, this is what I wrote:

"I am too stressed and worried about the state of my health. Much of the time whenever I experience a physical pain, I'm worried the pain will be chronic and I will feel it at all times. This all began when I was sick with the H-Pylori virus over two years ago. I developed acid reflux, and then one day I passed out while I was running. I had a heart rate of 24 (normal is 80-100) and no blood pressure. Matter of fact, the emergency room nurses thought their blood pressure monitor had broken. I found out the electrical system of my heart had stopped and it almost killed me. I run 25 miles per week and could tolerate a low heart rate. Others might have died, but through the gift of science, a heart pacemaker was installed and I haven't missed a beat yet. I then developed tinitus in my left ear, a painful kidney stone, a pinched nerve in my neck, a lipoma on my back, and a cracked root in one of my teeth. I want to be free of this preoccupation with health. This makes me feel hopeless at times and I have to push myself to overcome the sense of hoplessness. I do not accept that any of this pain has to be with me the rest of my life."

I found I could learn from all the Inquire Within exercises, but asking follow up questions in the Inquire Within Questionnaire was especially helpful to me.

One of the questions I created after my first go 'round with the program was…

How do I learn not to focus on my body pain so much and why do I fixate on these aches?

My answer:

"I've come to understand that all these physical ailments coming one after another felt overwhelming and would have been stressful for anyone. If I acknowledge this fact, I stop beating up on myself and let go of this fear/angst. I believe these health issues have led to me having post traumatic stress disorder. Now that I accept this, I am more understanding of the preoccupation with aches and pains. I feel I have improved, because now when I feel an ache or pain in my body I pay attention to it as little as possible. I figure if it's a serious issue, I'll deal with it later and not go into denial. Previously when I felt a twinge in my back or a pull in my hip, I would immediately panic and truly believe this pain was going to be present forever. I have moved dramatically away from this way of thinking and feeling. I also obtain regular massages, exercise and stretch regularly, and take vitamins and supplements. I try to appreciate my good fortune. I have been happily married for almost forty years; I have a great private psychotherapy practice; I'm an author of three critically acclaimed books, am a percussionist, and an athlete."

NOTES

Chapter 9

Celebration Stories

Most of the people who used the Inquire Within Program have faced, worked through, and overcome difficult struggles. Each of them experienced trauma and emotional wounds that carried long-lasting effects. Each was socially isolated at specific times in their lives. Each suffered from low self-esteem and lack of confidence. Each had problems trusting others and having faith in their own process. Each of them endured feelings of depression and anxiety. And each had trouble developing a framework for getting unstuck.

I'd like to share a few of these stories with you. In the beginning of therapy, I do most of the questioning. When my clients begin to employ Inquire Within, they model my questions as a way to ask their own. In these celebration stories, I'm going to show some of the questions I asked the clients, along with their answers, and then follow this with some of the questions and answers they reached while using Inquire Within.

~ ~ ~ ~

~Lois~

Lois is a 35-year-old white woman who initially came into my office because she was having problems sleeping and was unhappy with her partner, whom she married three years earlier. She is administrator of a nonprofit agency that helps homeless youth. When Lois first saw me, she complained that she once loved her job, but now felt it was enervating to open her office door each morning.

My Questions

Question:

This is your first meeting with me. What brings you into my office today?

Answer:

I'm feeling more tired than usual. I'm not excited by much. I don't see much of a future. I'm not happy with my husband, but I don't think the problem has anything to do with him. I think it's all about me. I don't believe I would be pleased with anyone right now.

Question:

Is anything else troubling you?

Answer:

Yes. I'm ashamed to say I've recently developed a temper. I became so angry at my husband that I threw a dish at him. Fortunately, I have bad aim and missed him, but the dish smashed into the kitchen wall. I've never had an anger problem before. I've always been able to control myself when I got mad, but not now.

Question:

> Has anything happened to you lately that may have been a triggering factor?

Answer:

> I've never told anyone, but about four years ago I was attacked by a man who pretended to be my friend. He used to work with me and we had been friendly for years. I've been to his house alone on numerous occasions. One night I dropped something over at his house and he raped me. I never told anyone about this because I was so ashamed. This man moved out of the city shortly after the incident. I don't know where he is and I don't want to know.

Question:

> That was very brave of you to share this with me – a therapist and a man. I'm honored you feel safe enough to open up to this extent. It seems you're carrying a lot of shame. Why do you think that is?

Answer:

> I am so embarrassed, humiliated, and ashamed for doing bad things...

Question:

> Do you think it was your fault you were raped?

Answer:

> I shouldn't have been stupid enough to go to his house.

Question:

> But hadn't you been to his house many times before without incident?

Answer:

> Yes, but I still should have known...

Question:

> So you should have been able to predict the future?

Answer:

No, I guess not.

Over the course of several months, Lois went to a rape support group to supplement her individual therapy sessions. During this period I taught Lois how to ask her own emotional pain questions.

Lois's Questions

Self-Question:

Why do I seem to be filled with shame?

Self-Answer:

I've always had a huge sense of guilt that's tied in with shame. My father pretty much ignored me unless he was beating me up. My mother would manipulate my father so he would physically punish me. He used tree branches, his fists, and paddles to hit me until I would bleed. My mother would say to my father, "Lois didn't clean her room. She was too busy playing basketball with those rich kids across town." This indeed infuriated my working-class father who didn't believe I should be stepping out of my station. He would whip me and simultaneously remind me to not move out of my rightful place. He said I was getting too big for my britches.

Self-Question:

So what does this all have to do with my present life?

Self-Answer:

I guess I believed I had to be perfect. I had to be the best worker, the best wife, and the best student. Deep inside, I prayed that if I was perfect that my parents would stop hurting me. I just wanted to be accepted and loved, but I had neither. I have no idea what it actually means to be truly loved and accepted. Oh, I do believe people really love me, but I am so guarded I can't accept their love and respect. However, now I'm ready to learn how to accomplish this.

Outcome Summary

Lois has attended individual therapy sessions and a rape support group for more than a year now. She intends to continue this work, at least in the short term, because it has been so helpful. She plans to continue using the Inquire Within Program indefinitely because it has been so revealing to her. She has accomplished the following:

- She developed a great communication system with her husband who turned out to be her number one cheerleader.
- She decided to file charges against the man who raped her. Her friends are offering their complete support.
- She understands the price she paid for keeping the secret about the rape for so long and has pledged to never keep secrets again.
- She confronted her mother and father about their abuse. They have apologized, but that relationship is still a work in progress.
- She decided to work as a consultant to homeless programs, and she now feels more satisfied with her work than she ever before.

~ ~ ~ ~

~Elizabeth~

Next is Elizabeth, a 28-year-old white woman whose presenting problem was that she needed help because a good friend of hers committed suicide. She works as a human resources director in a large software company.

My Questions

Question:

> You said on the phone your friend committed suicide last month. Please tell me what happened.

Answer:

> Mona was a friend of mine since we were kids. We went to grade school together in San Francisco. She seemed to be doing fine. She had a nice boyfriend and loved her job. One day, she overdosed on prescription medication; I think it was Oxycotin or Vicodin. She left a note saying the pressure to succeed had become all too much and so she decided to end her life. She was only 27 years old.

Question:

> How does her suicide make you feel?

Answer:

> I feel sad and a real sense of loss. She was my best friend for such a long time. I am also confused and not at all clear why she did this. I probably shouldn't be saying it, but I'm angry she died this way. Couldn't she have tried to get some help?

Question:

> Elizabeth, I want to assure you that being angry at a close friend for killing herself is a normal feeling to have. Talk more about why you're so angry.

Answer:

> I sometimes think about how selfish she was to leave all of us behind. Her family and boyfriend are devastated. We may never get over this. What the hell was she thinking?

Question:

> Do you somehow feel responsible for what happened?

Answer:

> Yes. I feel very guilty because I didn't pick up on any signs that she was troubled. I had no idea she felt so pressured. It's

like I didn't ever really know her; I just thought I did. She had this whole dark side she was living in that she didn't share with anyone else.

Question:

Why do you think she hid this part of herself from her loved ones?

Answer:

I'm not really sure. My guess is that she was a perfectionist and couldn't tolerate having flaws. She always tried to measure up to these extreme, unrealistic standards that she created for herself.

Question:

Oftentimes the loss of a loved one can open up other painful memories. Are you currently experiencing any of those?

Answer:

When I was eight years old my parents divorced. That was in itself a shattering experience for me. It was also an incident where I had no clue what was going to occur until my mother told me my dad was moving out. Moving out is exactly what he did, and he never bothered to contact me again.

Although Elizabeth found the therapy process painful, she came to believe that if she continued working on herself she would find peace regarding the death of her friend and the abandonment by her father.

Elizabeth's Questions

Self-Question:

How do I feel about Mona's suicide?

Self-Answer:

I think I have come to terms with the fact that I'll never come up with a comforting reason why she killed herself.

I think I've learned to handle having all kinds of feelings about her all at once, which I wasn't able to do before. I love her, and yet I am deeply enraged at her. I have read her suicide note and it really doesn't reveal much except she felt she could never measure up to all the pressure on her. She never specified what that pressure was, so one is left to guess, and I'm tired of speculating. I don't think I will ever know why this tragic event happened.

Self-Question:

How did the abandonment of my father affect me?

Self-Answer:

When he first left my family, I was only eight years old. I loved him, but now I don't really have any substantial memories; nothing I can really hold on to and reminisce about dear old dad. Sometimes I think not having any connection with him is worse than anything I can imagine. I sometimes wonder what I might have done to make my father leave. I also sometimes think I must be a wretched person since he left me and never got back in touch. I don't have any idea where he is. I never had a dad to guide me and hold me. Therefore, I had no good or bad example of how men are supposed to be. This has caused me endless soul searching regarding how much crap I should put up with from a man. It also has me questioning what level of intimacy is reasonable to achieve with one.

Self-Question:

At this point, what do I really want in my life?

Self-Answer:

I do want a serious relationship. I hope to get married someday and have children. I want to have a job I love to go to each day. I want friends I can count on. I don't want to live inside the anxious part of my being. I want to hold my head up into the sun and not worry when darkness will befall me again. I have faith all this will happen.

Outcome Summary

Elizabeth continues to work on her issues regarding the suicide of Mona and the abandonment by her father. She also continues to use the Inquire Within Program. She has accomplished the following:

- She no longer blames herself for her father leaving her. She is not clear about his exact reasons for abandoning her, but she no longer obsesses over this issue.
- She organized a memorial for Mona one year after her death. Elizabeth was able to obtain peace of mind through this process.
- She has acquired tools that keep her from lingering in an anxious state.
- She has recently begun a new relationship where she is willing to risk being vulnerable. She is beginning to let down her guard.

~ ~ ~ ~

~Ben~

Ben is a 43-year-old African-American man who was referred to me by a close friend because his wife of fifteen years had been killed in a plane accident. He is the father of two girls, ages 15 and 13. When he came to me, he complained of being fearful much of the time, having suicidal thoughts, difficulty concentrating, and finding his life purposeless. He feels alone and isolated. The first time I saw him was two weeks after his wife's death.

My Questions

Question:

I'm so sorry for what happened to your wife. I can only imagine how overwhelming it has been for you.

Answer:

There are times when I don't really accept that she died. She was here one day when I drove her to the airport and then – bam – the plane has a malfunction and crashes into a field in Kansas. It is just so surreal that I feel life has become a dream for me. No, not a dream – a nightmare.

Question:

Do you have a support system; folks you can talk to when you're feeling down?

Answer:

I can talk to my daughters, but I don't want to burden them with my grief. My friends and coworkers at the gym will listen to me, but I don't want to bother them either.

Question:

So you're a very independent man who doesn't want to rely on anyone for anything.

Answer:

That pretty much sums it up. But now is different from two weeks ago when my wife Jane died. I have never felt so all alone in my life. I have no buffer. I want to hear her voice. I want to smell her and I want to hold her. I don't know what I'm going to do.

Question:

I know you aren't going to believe what I'm about to say, but I'll say it anyhow. You will feel better in time and you will find a way to live without Jane. It won't be easy; no, the opposite is true. This will probably be the most painful journey you have ever experienced. You will find your grief will not have much pattern to it. It's more like the dips in a roller coaster ride where you have extreme ups and downs. My job is to help you through this process and I believe I can do so.

Answer:

I believe you can help me as well. Thanks for not sugar-coating it and saying this is all God's will. I don't really believe in God right now. If a god existed, why would he take my wife from this earth? There is no rationale for this.

Question:

So Ben, you feel like you've lost your faith? Do you think about joining your wife?

Answer:

Yes, sometimes I desperately want to join her wherever she may be. But I really can't consider killing myself. I'm responsible for taking care of my daughters, and if I died it would devastate my girls. I would never put them through that.

Question:

I'm glad you have reasons to continue living. How are you sleeping and eating?

Answer:

I don't have much of an appetite. I used to run six miles a day, four days a week, but now I don't have the motivation to move my body at all. I fall asleep easily, but wake up a 3 a.m. on the dot without hope of falling back asleep. I think about Jane and all I've lost. I cry buckets of tears.

Question:

Are you working right now?

Answer:

No, I'm not. Do you think I should? So many of my friends and family think I should go back to work immediately, but I'm not so sure.

Question:

Everyone grieves differently. Some find the distraction of work to be a good focus rather than feeling they're dwelling on the loss. Other people can't conceive of working and need time to feel and process the pain. You have the right to try working or not. It's totally up to you. What would you like to do? Do you have to work right now?

Answer:

I do need to work to have some cash flowing in. I also need a reason to wake up in the morning, so I'll give work a try.

Ben's Questions

Self-Question:

How am I feeling about my wife's death?

Self-Answer:

I miss her so much. I realize that at this point I've put her on a pedestal where she is the image of perfection. She was not perfect; no one is. Some friends are encouraging me to date, but it has only been a short time since she died, and I have no desire for a primary relationship. Do I get lonely? Sure I do, and sometimes the pain is unbearable, but at this point I know I will get through this agony and land in a neutral mindset where nothing is exciting or meaningful. However, I'm not screaming in the night either. I still cannot imagine my life without Jane. She was my best friend and loved me unconditionally. I don't believe I can ever attain that again. I do believe that in my recovery I will discover something that will make my life more peaceful.

Outcome Summary

Ben has now joined a grief support group and finds it tremendously helpful. He regularly uses the Inquire Within Program and is increasingly confident in his ability to work through the loss of his wife. He has achieved the following:

- He is now able to genuinely be there for his daughters. They now feel comfortable talking about the loss of their mother with him. They were reluctant to bring up their mom previously, because they realized their dad was heavily into his own mourning.
- He has started exercising again, and that helps him to feel more positive about the future.
- He noticed there are times during the day when he isn't focusing on the loss of Jane.
- He realizes he's living more in the present. Now, a year since his wife's accident, he can see the possibility of having another relationship.
- He has regained his sense of faith and has decided to join a church in his neighborhood.

Conclusion

You have completed reading this book and now you're ready to start the Inquire Within Program. Turn back to page 113 and begin this wonderful journey.

As you work through the questions and answers that will take you on an emotional journey, I welcome your comments and questions. You may contact me at *bobl@boblivingstone. com* and check out my webpage at *www.boblivingstone.com*.

NOTES

About the Author

*B*ob Livingstone, Licensed Clinical Social Worker (LCSW) has been a psychotherapist treating children, teens, and adults in the San Francisco Bay area for twenty-four years. He is the author of two critically acclaimed books. Midwest Book Review called *Redemption of the Shattered: A Teenager's Healing Journey through Sandtray Therapy* (Booklocker, 2002) "profound." *The Body Mind Soul Solution: Healing Emotional Pain*

through Exercise (Pegasus 2007) received rave reviews from New York Times-bestselling author Anne Louise Gittleman, The Saint Louis Post Dispatch, The Miami Herald, The Indianapolis Star, and Library Journal.

He has been featured in CNN.com, ABCNews.com, The New York Daily News.com, The Associated Press, The Dallas Morning News, The Hartford Courant, The Miami Herald, The Saint Louis Post-Dispatch, USA Today, MSNBC, WCBStv.com, The San Francisco Chronicle, MSN, The Christian Science Monitor, The Detroit Free Press.com, The Chicago Tribune, Natural Health magazine, Library Journal, Grand magazine, Positive Thinking magazine, Boston.com, Lee's Summit Journal, The Athens Banner-Herald, OregonLive.com, San Francisco Examiner.com, Martha Stewart's Satellite Radio Network, AOL Canada, WebMd and Womansday.com.

Bob Livingstone's written articles have been published in DrLaura.com, Beliefnet.com, Sheknows.com, Ediets.com, Selfgrowth.com, Care2.com, Memory-of.com, Lovetoknowkids.com, The Therapist Magazine, MentalHelp.net and Psychotherapy.net.

Available from NorlightsPress and fine booksellers everywhere

Toll free: 888-558-4354   **Online:** www.norlightspress.com
Shipping Info: Add $2.95 - first item and $1.00 for each additional item

Name _____

Address _____

Daytime Phone _____

E-mail _____

No. Copies	Title	Price (each)	Total Cost

Subtotal	
Shipping	
Total	

Payment by (circle one):
   Check   Visa   Mastercard   Discover   Am Express

Card number_____3 digit code_____

Exp.date_____ Signature_____

Mailing Address:
> 762 State Road 458
> Bedford IN 47421

Sign up to receive our catalogue at
www.norlightspress.com

33661931R00090

Made in the USA
Lexington, KY
07 July 2014